LIBRARY-BASED FAMILY LITERACY PROJECTS

Margaret Monsour
and
Carole Talan

American Library Association
Chicago and London 1993

Cover designed by Charles Bozett

Text designed by Dianne M. Rooney

Composition by Charles Bozett

Printed on 50-pound Finch Opaque, a pH-neutral stock, and bound in 10-point C1S by IPC, St. Joseph, MI

The paper used in this publication meets the minimum requirements of American National Standard for Information Sciences—Permanence of Paper for Printed Library Materials, ANSI Z39.48–1984. ∞

Library of Congress Cataloging-in-Publication Data

Monsour, Margaret.
   Library-based family literacy projects / by Margaret Monsour and Carole Talan.
     p. cm.
   ISBN 0-8389-0610-9 (alk. paper)
   1. Libraries and new literates—United States. 2. Family literacy programs—United States. 3. Public libraries—United States—Services to the illiterate. I. Talan, Carole. II. Title.
Z716.45.M66 1993
027.6—dc20   92-41088

Copyright © 1993 by the American Library Association. All rights reserved except those which may be granted by Sections 107 and 108 of the Copyright Revision Act of 1976.

Printed in the United States of America.

97 96 95 94 93   5 4 3 2 1

Contents

Preface   v

Introduction   ix

Bell Atlantic/ALA Family Literacy Project   1

    Milton, Delaware, Sussex County Department of Libraries   3
        PARTY (Parents Actively Reading to Youth)

    Fairmont, West Virginia, Marion County Public Library   9
        My Mom and Me

    Lexington, Virginia, Rockbridge Regional Library   14
        Grow Your Own Readers

    Pittsburgh, Pennsylvania, Carnegie Library of Pittsburgh   19
        Read Together

    Newport News, Virginia, Newport News Public Library   24
        Newport News Public Library

    Huntington, West Virginia, Cabell County Public Library   29
        Project LIFT (Literacy Involves Families Working Together)

California's Families for Literacy   35

    Long Beach   37

    National City   43

    Santa Barbara   48

    San Rafael   54

    Contra Costa   59

    Redwood City   64

Conclusion   71

Preface

Library-based Family Literacy Projects is a directory of library-based family literacy programs. The public library connection to family literacy is becoming stronger throughout the country and owes its viability to two initiatives: the Bell Atlantic/ALA Family Literacy Project and the Families for Literacy program. This work describes 12 outstanding programs that are currently in operation.

The Bell Atlantic/ALA Family Literacy Project

The Bell Atlantic/ALA Family Literacy Project, established in 1989 and funded by the Bell Atlantic Foundation, is administered by the American Library Association's Office of Library Outreach Services (OLOS). It is a regional project centered in the mid-Atlantic states of Virginia, West Virginia, New Jersey, Delaware, Pennsylvania, Maryland, and the District of Columbia. The goal of the project is to encourage solutions to the problem of low-literacy by developing local partnerships in communities among libraries, adult basic education specialists and literacy providers, and a local business partner and through the implementation of library-based family literacy programs.

In 1989 Bell Atlantic approached the American Library Association to join with them to develop a literacy project. The idea of family literacy was identified by a steering committee of library leaders from the mid-Atlantic states mentioned above, who met to discuss how to design a program administered by public libraries that would serve the needs of adults and children and strengthen the reading skills of family members.

Since 1990 the project has funded a total of 58 family literacy projects in 45 communities. Twenty-five projects were funded the first year with grants of $5,000. In the second year, 12 projects received continued funding and 13 new projects were begun, again with grants of $5,000. In the third year, 14 projects were funded with grants up to $10,000, including eight new locations and four matching grants for up to as much as $5,000 for existing programs. With a third grant to the American Library Association in 1992 of $500,000, the project will continue through December 1994. Total funding received from Bell Atlantic is over 1 million dollars.

From the American Library Association's perspective, this project serves as a model for public libraries nationwide to show what can be done working cooperatively with other community agencies. It also demonstrates how to develop library-based family literacy projects and provides evidence that a not-for profit institution can cooperate with the private sector to develop a viable program that meets the goals of both organizations.

Bell Atlantic is involved in this partnership to develop a regional project that has national implications. It has concentrated on a region of the country that it serves to try and improve the reading skills of the people in communities who will eventually become part of the local workforce. The project is a call to action for other corporate leaders to enter the literacy arena and to join with other nonprofit organizations. The impact of the project may be even more significant 15 years from now when participants in the current family literacy projects become members of the workforce.

California's Families for Literacy

In California the needs of "at risk" families are being addressed through the Families for Literacy (FFL) program. Begun in 1988 through legislation sponsored by Senator David Roberti, this program provides state local assistance funds each year to local libraries already offering adult literacy services (primarily through the state-funded California Literacy Campaign). Funds are used to develop family literacy programs for adults already a part of the adult literacy program who have at least one pre-school child. In fiscal year 1991–92, the fourth year of the program,

28 FFL programs received individual grants ranging from $4,000 to $30,000. Two FFL programs, in Napa and Pasadena, after two years of state support are continuing family literacy services with local support.

Half of California's 168 library jurisdictions provide direct adult literacy instruction to their communities through the California Literacy Campaign (CLC), also known since passage of legislation in 1990 as the California Library Literacy Service (CLLS). The CLC is the first statewide, state-funded public library operated literacy instructional program in the nation. Its purpose is to provide free, one-on-one basic literacy tutoring to English-speaking adults who are unable or unwilling to seek help through traditional Adult Basic Education (ABE). Since 1984 the CLC has offered financial assistance as well as technical support to those library jurisdictions wishing to provide literacy services.

An innovative leader in library-based literacy, the CLC has developed its own learner assessment system and its own database for recording and reporting data about its programs. The California Adult Learner Progress Evaluation Process (CALPEP) tracks the progress of the adult learner from entry into a program until exit. It follows a self-assessment model which includes effective assessments such as how the learner perceives his or her reading and writing ability, how often he or she participates in a variety of reading or writing activities, and what his or her reading and writing goals are. CALPEP is also used to track family literacy activities and changes in attitudes and skills by both parents and children.

Each California literacy program has developed unique characteristics based on community needs and on the individuals who are involved in the delivery of services. Similar in many ways, the programs are also different in many other ways.

Space does not allow a full description of all of the family literacy programs in California, but six programs with unusual approaches, features, or innovations are included here.

Both of these programs, the Bell Atlantic/ALA Family Literacy Project and California's Families for Literacy, have succeeded in developing alliances and partnerships that illustrate the strength of collaborations with the public library. These partnerships use the resources and expertise from many organizations to demonstrate that established local community agencies, the public library, the adult basic education program, literacy councils, and local businesses can successfully work together and develop family literacy programs that will help break the inter-generational cycle of low literacy.

MARGARET MONSOUR

Introduction

This publication has several purposes: to report on library-based family literacy projects and their development as a legitimate approach to the problem of low literacy, to present model programs and discuss their components, to identify program ideas that may be replicated in libraries throughout the country, and to encourage the expansion of a network of family literacy program providers.

Low literacy contributes to an ongoing cycle of educational disadvantage, frustration, poverty and dependence. There is growing awareness that adult low literacy can and must be addressed through the family as well as through the broader community. Research indicates the two major characteristics of low literacy: it is cyclical and inter-generational. Children who grow up in an environment of books and reading tend to become good readers, while those who grow up without family support for reading do not. A supportive family setting not only gives a child the opportunity to develop reading skills, but also gives reading a practical value in a social context. The family literacy concept reflects the fact that literacy, the ability to read and to understand, begins at home.

What Is Family Literacy?

Family literacy is a shared learning experience that strengthens the family and provides an opportunity for adults to improve basic skills and for children to develop a love of books and an early understanding of reading. A bond created between parents and children working toward a common goal is a powerful incentive to change behavior and to break the cycle of low literacy. Family literacy programs help improve adult literacy, increase reading skills or reading readiness for children, and foster good reading habits for each family member. Family literacy programs include these three elements:

1. Literacy and parenting education and instruction for adults
2. Pre-reading and other literacy activities for children
3. Time for parents to use their new skills with their children

The projects profiled in this book include these elements and individual project descriptions illustrate how these components are developed within the structure of each program. Many factors, including the community partners, the target population, availability of resources, and additional circumstances determine the scope of these family literacy programs.

Modeling by service providers and librarians is a very important component of every family literacy program because it presents parents with a different way of relating to their children. Modeling can include showing parents how to "read" a book which may have no words, how to interest young children in shapes and colors, and how to use rhyme to help children develop language skills. The most important part of family literacy occurs when parents and children come together and interact with each other. That's when the learning transfer begins and the cycle is broken.

The following are examples of activities that are part of family literacy programs:

> Programs that include low literate parents, or other family members and children and that increase the communication skills of participants in the program. Improving parenting skills of the adults, developing reading readiness skills in children, teaching parents how to relate to their children by sharing books and stories together, and modeling reading and storytelling behavior are some of the ways that communication skills are enhanced through family literacy programs.

> Services that include cooperation in planning educational activities for families where members are seeking to reach functional literacy, for example, recruitment and training of volunteers, teaching library skills to the target audience, or the development of new reader collections.

Family literacy programs are built on collaboration among existing community agencies and the library. Adult basic education (ABE) providers in the community, which often include the local library, offer literacy services for the adult learner. The children's librarian provides reading activities for children and also models positive reading behavior for parents. Using the resources of existing community service providers makes sense because it reduces duplication of efforts to reach the same target population and expands services to families who may already be receiving support. For example, many library-based family literacy project planners develop partnerships with Chapter 1 teachers or Head Start staff. Parents and children already enrolled in these programs can then be introduced to the library and experience the pleasure of sharing activities with their children and learn to enjoy reading with their children through a library-based family literacy project. To illustrate another possibility for collaboration, many adults enrolled in ABE programs or literacy tutoring programs such as Literacy Volunteers of America (LVA) are also parents. Developing a partnership with an adult literacy provider may mean holding classes in the library and while adults receive individual tutoring, the children participate in a storytime. Bringing parents and children together in a positive family activity in the library and encouraging family members to develop new skills completes the circle of collaboration and reinforces the concept that the parents' role is critical in their child's development and that reading can be fun for every member of the family.

Collaboration and cooperation among agencies are essential for a successful family literacy project. Partners in family literacy projects may include: Head Start, local school districts, family shelters for battered women, social service agencies, well-baby clinics, Department of Employment Security, LVA (Literacy Volunteers of America), local banks, service clubs, literacy councils, hospitals, bookstores, and universities and many others.

Libraries and the Literacy Connection

Why family literacy in the library? Because that's where the books are! Families who are economically disadvantaged do not have many books and some may have no books at all. At the library, parents and children select books to take home and enjoy together. When family literacy programs are held elsewhere, most of the children never go to the library with their parents, especially in rural communities where transportation is difficult and expensive. At the library, children and adults can find books on similar subjects or genres, thus encouraging family discussions. Unlike schools and most social programs, families have full access to books and other library materials such as videos and books on tape. Getting to know the library becomes a part of the life of all family members, no matter what the age or economic status.

Librarians have a long history of promoting literature through book-related programs, and family literacy programs incorporate many services and activities that are traditional in libraries. As an information and service organization, the library is a natural focal point for family literacy. The public library, with its mission to serve the general public, already offers children's programming, literacy materials, literacy instruction, and literacy support services. In many libraries, literacy providers have already established tutoring space for adults in the library. With the addition of a family literacy program in the library, both parents and children can benefit from individual and shared learning experiences in a relaxed and pleasant atmosphere. Family literacy is a natural way to bring adult literacy and children's services together to reach the target population of these most "at risk" families.

National attention on family literacy has provided librarians with opportunities to augment networks and resources and to share educational efforts within the community. Librarians can take a leadership role by providing family literacy programs that focus on parents and children. The model projects in this book illustrate how librarians in large urban libraries, suburban library systems, and small rural libraries are expanding existing programs and initiating family literacy programs in their communities.

Family Literacy Program Models: The Bell Atlantic/ALA Family Literacy Project

The partnership concept is at the center of the Bell Atlantic/ALA Family Literacy Project. The librarian is the project team coordinator and an adult basic education specialist or literacy provider forms part of the family literacy project team. The third team member is an employee volunteer from Bell Atlantic. This business team member brings a unique perspective to the family literacy projects, helps create new alliances among the existing community agencies, and strengthens the coalition.

Family literacy programs have a significant influence on the business community because they encourage children and adults to develop reading skills in the home that help break the inter-generational cycle of low literacy. The reading skills gained or enhanced in family literacy programs are transferred to the workplace creating a more literate and productive community.

The business partner may play a variety of roles during the project development. Here are some suggested ways business people may participate in a library-based family literacy program.

Contribute Professional Support

Contribute time to help the literacy project develop a strong business connection within the community.

Help community organizations write proposals or seek grants.

Provide in-kind assistance to local literacy programs including space to hold classes, donations of computers and other equipment, and printing of instructional materials.

Provide Program Support

Contact other community agencies to gain support for the family literacy project.

Become a tutor for adults.

Help recruit other volunteer tutors.

Be a volunteer reader for children.

Help with transportation in rural communities.

Create Public Awareness

Contact local businesses or business organizations and offer to contribute an article about the library's family literacy projects to the company newsletter.

Be an advocate for literacy. Participate in local literacy coalitions.

The Bell Atlantic/ALA Family Literacy project has three distinct components:

1. a grants program
2. training for grant recipients
3. a resource service offered through the American Library Association

The grants program awards grants up to $5,000 (1990–92) and $10,000 (1992–94) to public libraries within the mid-Atlantic region. Grant recipients participate in a two-day training seminar to sharpen and expand skills that will be used in the development of their family literacy program. A resource service, maintained by the American Library Association, publishes and distributes family literacy fact sheets to libraries across the country, has developed a nationwide literacy newsletter database, and collects information about other family literacy projects across the country.

An important requirement of these library-based family literacy project grants is a training workshop which must be planned and implemented by the project team coordinator and the family literacy project staff. The workshop is also presented to other community agencies, and has been a significant factor in drawing the community into the activity of the family literacy project. Presenting the workshop strongly encourages librarians to be proactive as visible advocates for family literacy and the library. The workshops strive to:

> Increase participants' awareness and understanding of the low literacy crisis and its consequences for families and communities
>
> Provide participants with resources for developing family literacy programs including the library's experience as a demonstration site and published sources
>
> Introduce participants to techniques that will enable them to:
> provide parent/child reading assistance in a variety of contexts
> access existing programs
> advocate creative educational programs for family literacy needs

During the first year of the project, the average attendance at training workshops among the 25 projects was 15, which means that 375 service providers in Virginia, West Virginia, Delaware, New Jersey, Pennsylvania, Maryland, and the District of Columbia have learned about the Bell Atlantic/ALA Family Literacy Project. In many of the projects, including Lebanon Public Library (Lebanon, Pa.), Monroe County Public Library (Union, W.Va.), Carnegie Library (Pittsburgh, Pa.), and Wilmington Library (Wilmington, Del.) to mention just a few, the project team coordinators also presented workshops at regional and state literacy associations, expanding the influence of the project well beyond the local community.

In many projects, agencies that were involved in the beginning brought in other agencies that shared in the current project and now plan to help continue and expand the project in the years to come. As an example, the Department of Health and Human Resources, Community Services, and Head Start referred parents to the Library Literacy Project for Parents (LIPPS) program at the Monroe County Public Library, in Union, W. Va. And although not originally identified as cooperating agencies, the Extension Homemaker Clubs provided lunches and snacks and the Lions Club provided free eyeglasses to several students. Also as a result of this project, the Monroe County schools began holding adult basic education classes in the library. Now there is an opportunity to tutor parents in conjunction with the adult literacy classes and families can enjoy being together and get the help they need at the library.

The initial 25 family literacy projects were completed in June 1991 and six libraries were recognized as outstanding models of library-based family literacy projects. These six projects are profiled in this book. They represent a variety of approaches toward family literacy and illustrate the impact of collaborative efforts in these communities. The six libraries include Cabell County Public Library (Huntington, W. Va.), Milton Public Library (Sussex County, Del.), Newport News Public Library (Newport News, Va.), Marion County Public Library (Fairmont, W. Va.), Rockbridge Regional Library (Rockbridge, Va.), and Read Together and the Beginning with Books program at the Carnegie Library (Pittsburgh, Pa.).

The Bell Atlantic/ALA Family Literacy Project is helping people who want to change behaviors to develop a different approach toward themselves and a different way to interact with their family members and within their communities. The participants in these projects took the opportunity to initiate and encourage changes in behavior and this is the greatest impact of the project—and also the most challenging and rewarding. Family members, adults, children, grandchildren have been introduced to reading and books and encouraged to develop a lifelong relationship with a community resource that belongs to them, their public library. Service providers, including adult literacy specialists, community agencies, and local businesses have increased their level of cooperation with each other and with the public library, which continues to play a leadership role in the development of strong coalitions within the local communities.

All of the projects developed individual evaluation plans for their libraries depending on specific goals for the project in their community. During the first year standardized data were not collected, but such data are required for the subsequent years of the project. However, it is possible through anecdotal information to gauge the impact of the project on family members. A brief anecdote from the Monroe County Library (Union, W. Va.) illustrates one incident:

> The metamorphosis in the parents is astounding. When parents first enter the program, they universally report bad school experiences. They are apprehensive, dormant. After a few weeks in the program they come to life and begin to participate. One of the parents, Pam, was terrified the first time she came. She was visibly shaking. She had to quit her job because they wanted to promote her to a super-

visory position. She certainly couldn't tell her employer that she couldn't read. She had been married for fourteen years before she even told her husband she couldn't read.

She had a sixteen year old son that wanted to quit school and a three year old son, David, that she knew she couldn't help. Now, she reports that she can't even sit down to try to read her homework without David wanting her to read to him. Reading to David is something she never thought she would be able to do.

And from the Fauquier County Library (Warrenton, Va.):

A family touched by the project are residents of some of the long-term Temporary Family Shelter Homes. This family, on attending Family Reading Night at the library, received library cards, made possible by a new temporary card policy which is an outcome of this project. The mother in this family was referred to a GED tutor and is making progress in her work towards that goal. And the family came back to the library on their own when their first books were due and enrolled their son and two neighbor children in our summer reading club.

Family Literacy Program Models: California's Families for Literacy

California's Families for Literacy program is a library service program which provides, among other activities, reading preparation services for young children in public library settings and instructs parents in reading aloud to their children. Its intention is not to have parents teach their children to read, but to recognize and foster the vital role that parents can play in preparing children for a lifetime of enjoyment and success in reading. Additionally, the program provides technical assistance, parent support, and any resources and materials necessary for its implementation. An important element of the program is the provision for acquisition of books by each child in the family.

The minimum requirements for providing services with FFL funding include:

Providing books for ownership

Holding meetings in libraries and introducing the families to the resources and services available

Providing storytelling, word games, and other enjoyable reading-oriented activities for families

> Encouraging the use of children's books for tutoring and language experience stories from the family programs as adult literacy instructional materials
>
> Teaching parents how to select books and why to read aloud to children
>
> Providing services that enhance full family participation and that foster a family environment for reading
>
> Helping parents gain access to books on parenting, child care, health, nutrition, and education.

Although only 28 of the 84 California Literacy Campaign (CLC) libraries have state-funded FFL programs, a number of other CLC programs do have family literacy components which are supported through local funds, bringing the number participating in family literacy to more than one-half the total of CLC libraries. It is the goal of the FFL campaign to eventually have all CLC programs fully involved in family literacy.

California's Families for Literacy program has come a long way since its inception in 1988. Many questions about how to operate a library-based family literacy program have been answered through trial and error. It has also become increasingly clear that what works in one community does not necessarily work in another. FFL programs are required by law to provide certain specific services, but the different libraries have developed programs with elements which are also unique to their communities.

Each community must find what approach works best for its learners. Some programs work primarily through their tutors; some work primarily through special parenting programs and storytimes in the library; most find that a combination approach works best. Some FFL programs present their family storytimes/theme parties on Saturdays; some find that week days or evenings during the week work best; others have found they need to offer a variety of times and days as choices in order to achieve full participation from their eligible FFL families.

We do know, however, that the most successful programs are ones that form cooperative efforts with others in their communities. Even Start, Head Start, adult education, community colleges, local Laubach or LVA literacy organizations, other community-based organizations, child care councils, day care providers, local elementary schools, Rotary, Soroptomist, Altrusa, business, industry, labor—the list of partners and potential partners is almost limitless.

Some of the things we have learned during the four years of the Bell Atlantic/ALA Family Literacy Project and California Families for Literacy program are elements that should be considered in the design of any family literacy program.

Family Literacy Program Planning: Lessons Learned

Team Building. The library "team" approach is essential for a successful family literacy program. Defining roles and expectations sets the stage for solid communication as the program develops. Children's services, literacy services, and adult services staff must work together as a team. Each provides his or her regular services but the service is expanded to the specially targeted audience of the low literacy level adult with preschool children.

Within the Bell Atlantic/ALA Family Literacy project the business partner is an important team member. Planning and implementing the program at the local level with support from the business team member mean stronger community support after grant funding ends. As a member of the local literacy coalition, a business team member can present a strong case for continued support of family literacy programs. Businesses realize the benefits of a literate workforce because literacy translates into a safer environment for employees who can read, plus encouraging increased productivity.

In the FFL program, the tutor is an integral part of the program. He or she is important for reinforcement, encouragement, guidance, and actual use of family materials in the tutoring session. Tutors are encouraged to help the adult learner take the language experience stories used during tutoring sessions and use them with their children. They are also crucial in securing the initial "buy-in" of the family and in helping them to attend family sessions held in the library.

Recruitment. It is more difficult than originally thought to recruit adult learners with low literacy skills into family literacy programs. The reasons for this are varied, but some that have been suggested are:

> Parents that fit the FFL criteria must also contend with many other problems, such as unemployment or underemployment, single-parent households, etc. Making the additional commitment in time and energy needed for family literacy activities may appear to them as a luxury.

> These parents don't necessarily see the connection between their low literacy skills and future learning difficulties for their children. They view the school as the place where learning takes place and must be completely re-educated about the importance of the early years in developing language and pre-literacy skills. Their tutors are often not aware of this importance either, especially with respect to infants and pre-

schoolers. Adult learners are as concerned as any parent about the language development and readiness for reading in their children, but they lack both skill and confidence in this area. These parents do not perceive themselves as "teachers" of their young children and do not know how to make education and reading a primary value in their home.

Many of these parents fear public exposure of their lack of literacy skills and the accompanying social stigma. They want to seek help for their children but are reluctant to reveal themselves as adults with low literacy skills. Most parents want to help their children with the skills that lead to reading, but many are not prepared to improve their own literacy. Often their children are the parents' single source of positive self esteem and the children's needs are paramount; however, since these same parents lack self esteem in the area of reading and education they often will not seek this type of help for themselves.

Early in the program special attention should be addressed to the issue of helping adult learners feel comfortable in the library and developing the children's services staff's awareness and sensitivity to the adult learner and his or her needs.

To address these recruitment issues it is important to develop a clear plan for recruitment before or during the first three months of the program. The plan should define your "target families," such as teen parents, at-risk children, incarcerated parents, low-income families.

Recruitment techniques that have proven most effective include referrals from new and current adult learners into the family literacy program. Generally, the K-12 school setting is not the best place to recruit new adult learners. Community agency referrals are a more effective method as well as referrals from community leaders or friends and relatives of the target group. Develop a list of names and addresses of community people who can assist your program. Ideas for your list include: ministers and church groups, preschool teachers, manufacturing plant managers, banks, hospitals, Head Start teachers, support groups for abused children or spouses, and social service agencies. Including a book giveaway in the family literacy program has proven to be a very effective recruiting technique within the Bell Atlantic projects; a book giveaway is a requirement within the California Families program.

Planning for Children. There are two distinct and definable age groups of pre-schoolers when it comes to designing programs: those under the age of 3 and those between 3 and 5. The first group works best in the oral tradition of language, with nursery rhymes, finger plays, songs, lap jogs, tickles, board books, and very simple books. Those children aged 3 to 5 are ready for more sophisticated language activities, such as longer books, participation songs, and finger plays.

Programs should be designed to recognize that often many of the children of adult learners are developmentally younger than their age would indicate. For a 3- to 5-year-old audience, plan for shorter attention spans and behaviors more appropriate to the toddler stage and be prepared to vary your approach.

As more adult learners with pre-school children are recruited into FFL programs, a need for financial support for child care during the tutoring sessions may occur. Many programs are not prepared to deal with this.

Also plan to include and involve older siblings. Older children who have not been previously exposed to language activities often respond at lower developmental levels, thus making chronological age a less defining factor for this target group. Parents, too, usually find storytimes as much fun as their children and enjoy exposure to quality children's books.

Children's Literature. The quality of the literature is crucial when selecting books for programming and acquisition by families. Enjoyable reading for the whole family should include a varied selection of children's literature that considers the age of the child or children, ethnic or cultural diversity, and reading ability of the family or parent.

It is important to emphasize that family literacy stresses shared enjoyment of reading, *not* teaching young children to read, and that the adult's literacy skills can be improved through the use of children's materials. Family literacy programs help establish a strong foundation for the development of pre-literacy skills. Do not assume that adult learners are aware of the importance of pre-literacy skill building to later success in acquiring basic reading and writing skills.

Marketing and Publicity. Library staff should be very proactive in coalition building with other community agencies and should allow at least six weeks lead time between program publicity and the actual start time of the program. Publicizing the program through members of the coalition means information transfer—and that is the best model we can provide family members.

What a library titles a program is very important! Low literate parents are more likely to attend a program in the library if it is a party or has a special theme rather than a typical storytime. After all, reading is usually not something the parent has found pleasurable. They cannot imagine why they would want to bring their children to the library for such an activity.

Personal Contact (Follow-Up). A great deal of personal attention is needed for family literacy programs. Much one-on-one work, tutor and staff encouragement, and individual modeling for parents in how to read and relate to their children are involved. Personal phone calls to motivate learners to participate and to remind them to attend programs are just two such examples. The work here is very staff intensive but the payoff is in the fact that not just one person but the entire family benefits. Often the family is a large one and as many as five to ten individuals can be reached through the involvement of a single family.

Involvement in family literacy programming in the library clearly leads to the development of new behaviors on the part of the adult learner and his or her family. Program participants usually increase their library use and the ways they use the library.

Public Stake in Family Literacy. Everyone has a vested interest in family literacy. Often all that is needed to start a program is to provide community leaders with information about family literacy and how they can work cooperatively with their library. Developing a presentation about the program, whether it means making a phone call, speaking at the Chamber of Commerce, writing a brochure, or making a video, pays off with support from community leaders and increased visibility for the program.

Above all, libraries have learned that family literacy programming is enjoyable as well as essential to a long-term solution to our nation's illiteracy problem. Adults often become participants in literacy programs because of their concern about helping their children. But just helping the adult achieve functional literacy is not enough. Children, too, from birth on must be included if we are to break this continuing cycle.

MARGARET MONSOUR

BELL ATLANTIC/ ALA FAMILY LITERACY PROJECT

PARTY
Parents Actively Reading to Youth

Sussex County Department of Libraries
Milton Library
121 Union St.
Milton, DE 19968
Contact: Christel Shumate
(302) 855-7890

In Delaware, the Sussex County Department of Libraries and Milton Library developed PARTY (Parents Actively Reading to Youth), their family literacy project, with two other agencies, READ-ALOUD Delaware, a private not-for-profit volunteer-based program devoted to ensuring that all pre-school children in Delaware are read aloud to on a regular basis and an agency of the Delaware Coalition for Literacy, plus Casa San Francisco, a crisis intervention and emergency shelter center providing services to farm workers and non-English-speaking adults. Families with children from 3- to 10-years-old received invitations to attend three sets of workshops.

    This program is targeted to low-income families with parents who may not know how to read and who may not encourage their children to learn to read. Each workshop includes three sessions each and has the themes of Land, Air, and Sea. Books and activities are planned to correspond to the theme of the evening. Each session includes time for parent discussion, a children's activity time, and a family enrichment time. Families attending all three sessions receive a four-shelf bookcase, each child receives a hardback book, and parent and child each receive a year's subscription to a magazine. The project emphasizes parenting skills, provides the families with gift books and the bookcase they can keep to start their own home library. As Christel Shumate, project director, said, "Low-income families have to spend most of their money on food and other items they need. They really can't afford to

3

buy books. This is a chance for them." And it is a chance for parents to become better readers. The program encourages parents to read and share books with their children and it may give them the encouragement to develop stronger literacy skills through other programs in Sussex County. The project team provides referrals to other community agencies.

The PARTY program was used as a model for the Delmarva Rural Ministries Family Literacy Program, given for the Haitian community in Laurel, Delaware. PARTY was recognized by the lieutenant governor of Delaware in 1991 and received the state's Outstanding Adult/Family Literacy Achievement award.

Description and Approach

The Milton Library service area covers approximately 55 square miles and has an estimated population of 7,600. The area is primarily rural agricultural, and the food processing industry is a major employer. Many migrant workers who speak English as a second language live in the area surrounding Milton. Approximately 38 percent of the population are black and ethnic minorities. The target audience of this family literacy program includes low-income families with pre-school and primary grade children.

PARTY is an interactive parent-child workshop that encourages parental involvement in reading-related activities with their children. Parents and children attend three two-hour sessions to complete one workshop. Each session is divided into family storytime, parent discussion group, children's activity time, and family activity time. Family storytime establishes the central theme for each session and all art activities completed are based on the themes of Land, Air, and Sea.

The parent discussion group is a structured program adapted from the R.A.F.T. (Reading Aloud Is Fun Together) outline developed by READ-ALOUD Delaware. The sessions run about 25 minutes and are intended to encourage parents to talk about their children, to think about enjoyable ways to foster some good reading habits in their family, and to recognize their own role in encouraging their child's success. Here is a sampling of how the parent group leader uses the R.A.F.T. materials to lead the parent discussion.

Session 1: Why Read?

Question for Discussion: Why share books with children?

Important Points: Learning to read gives our children power and gives our children a way to find out about the world. It strengthens our bond with our children.

Session 2: Cooperation and Listening

Question for Discussion: Are these (cooperation and listening) ever a problem at your house? (Parents always get going on this one!) What works? What doesn't work?

Important Points: Using praise, mutual respect, giving undivided attention. The goal is inspired listening vs. artificial listening.
 The group leader may suggest games for improving listening, such as imitating animal sounds and other sounds in the environment and making up silly rhymes.

Parent Exercise: Pair up and "read" wordless books to each other.

Session 3: Conversation Skills/Getting Ready to Read

Questions for Discussion: How can we develop conversations with our kids? How can we teach some basic concepts?

Important Points: Children have many ways of talking; tears, hugs, questioning, playing. Conversation is crucial to language development and a child's visual skill. Show and Tell is an example of a simple game to use. Basic concepts can be taught by using items right from the home (e.g., sock match-up and count the eggs in the carton). Teaching basic concepts develops a child's visual skill, an important pre-reading skill.

Parent Exercise: Develop conversation skills to use with children. In the parent group, each person tells the worst thing that happened to them that day, then the best thing. The group leader suggests that parents tell their children the worst and the best of their day and then ask their child if he or she has a worst and best thing to share too.

Methods and Materials

The three workshops are scheduled to include both separate and cooperative activities for parents and children. The beginning of each is devoted to a family storytime; parents and children then separate. Parents receive activity sheets to be used with their children and participate in exercises and in role-playing demonstrating positive ways of interacting with their children. During this time children meet with a group leader separate from parents for creative and fun activities. Retired Senior Volunteer Program (RSVP) volunteers and READ-ALOUD Delaware volunteers read to the children and help with child care and craft activities. After a short break, the program resumes with parents and children working together on craft activities and practicing skills they have learned earlier in the class.

When this family literacy project began, trying to find the right time to schedule the workshops was quite a challenge. The program planners agree that flexibility is critical for the success of the program. During the course of this project, workshop dates and scheduled times had to be adjusted each time. Initially, the workshops were planned for 1-1/2 hours on Wednesday at 6:30 p.m. But that was too early for working parents and the time period was too short. The second workshop was scheduled for 2 hours on Wednesday morning, but that was an awkward time for the target audience. The third workshop was held on Saturday from noon to 2 p.m. and this seemed to work the best.

Personnel

Christel Shumate, Sussex County Department of Libraries for Milton Library, is project team coordinator. Other team members include Anne Child from Casa San Francisco, Ryan Brown from READ-ALOUD Delaware and Lewes Reeves from Diamond State Telephone.

Recruitment and Cooperating Agencies

Recruitment for the workshops is done through H.O. Brittingham Elementary Special Education and Chapter 1 classes, Milton Day Care, and Indian River Adult Education. Fliers in both Spanish and English are distributed door-to-door in developments and stress program incentives that include free bookcases, new children's books, magazine subscriptions, and craft materials.

Fliers in Spanish and English are also distributed through the ABE-GED Adult Education and Parent-Child Development programs at Casa San Francisco and local food processing plants. Referrals are made from public housing developments and potential participants are contacted individually.

Lewes Reeves, manager of community relations for Diamond State Telephone and the Bell Atlantic employee volunteer, contributed his support to the program. Reeves is very active in the community and serves on a number of local boards. He helped publicize the project to other organizations and through his involvement encouraged other people to participate in literacy programs.

In addition to the agencies already mentioned, Milton Volunteer Fire Department donated plastic rulers for every child. Graystone Equipment and Rental Company donated John Deere Storybook Series for Little Folks to the program as giveaway books to families. Other Sussex County libraries provided plastic bags for each child to keep supplies in. Bookcases were purchased at cost.

Costs

Coordinator	$ 932
Consultant services	1,654
Child care	36
Magazine subscriptions	521
Books	288
Bookcases	636
Mini-collection	564
Videos	33
Supplies	146
Transportation	190
Total	$5,000

In-kind contributions were received from the Milton Library, R.A.F.T., the Volunteer Fire Department, and the trustees of the Library Board that equal $3,840. Total cost of the project was $8,840.

Support Services

Milton Library provides tutoring space for Project READS, which is the Sussex County Department of Libraries literacy program. The library acts as a referral center for Project READS, maintains an adult new reader collection, and provides promotional assistance.

Special Services

As a follow-up to PARTY, the Milton Library provided seven programs for the Casa San Francisco youth program in addition to the regular storyhours at the library. The children attending these programs were allowed to check out books using the Casa San Francisco staff library card, enabling them to participate in the 1991 summer reading program which would otherwise not have been available to most of them.

My Mom and Me

Marion County Public Library
321 Monroe St.
Fairmont, WV 26554
Contact: Cheryl Kuykendall
(304) 366-8142

North Central (WV) Opportunities Industrialization Center (OIC) is a local job training and education program that was funded in 1989 by the State Department of Education to operate a family literacy project in Marion County, West Virginia. The project is titled "My Mom and Me" and it focuses on breaking the inter-generational dependence on the welfare system by helping mothers overcome personal obstacles to employment and emphasizing the role of mother as first teacher.

In 1990, OIC joined forces with its next door neighbor, the Marion County Public Library, to add a needed component to the My Mom and Me program. These two very different agencies, established for different reasons, identified a common goal: to provide literacy and educational services for the same population of parents and pre-school children. A survey of participants in the literacy project revealed that none of the families currently used library services on a regular or semi-regular basis. Additionally, none of the participants were aware of the library's educational activities and resources, such as materials for low level readers, children's storyhour, the summer reading program, or literacy support services.

The project's target population is low income women with children under school age who are most in need of literacy training, remedial education, and job training services. Motivation for literacy is enhanced through experience with a positive educational environment which focuses on the needs of the entire family. The project also provides exposure to and awareness of library activities. Library resources are identified to encourage parents to increase and develop their own reading skills and to foster good reading habits as a family-centered activity.

Cheryl Kuykendall and Lynette Orbivich from My Mom and Me both emphasized the tremendous impact of the mother as a positive role model. "When children see their mothers changing—when the mother goes to school and starts working, when she presents learning and reading as enjoyable and fun things to do—the child will follow." The cycle will be broken and the circle of community opened to these new learners.

Description and Approach

Marion County Library is located in Fairmont, West Virginia and serves a population of 66,000. Two branches are located in the rural communities of Fairview and Mannington. The region's economy is based largely on manufacturing and coal mining.

Marion County, like most of West Virginia, has suffered from a recessionary economy for most of the last 10 years. The unemployment rate is 10 percent. During the 1980s Marion County was designated by the Secretary of Labor as a laborer surplus area because of its persistently high unemployment.

The approach of the family literacy program is to recruit "at-risk" parents and their pre-school children and to provide a family centered educational program that addresses the issue of undereducation, poverty, and low literacy.

Developing a program to help change the attitude of parents toward education is an ambitious goal. My Mom and Me identified this goal and has focused its program on helping women develop social, communication, and problem-solving skills.

Parents with their pre-school age children attend classes three days a week, two hours per day at a nearby center. The first hour of the day, the children participate in a pre-school program designed to promote a positive learning experience. Meanwhile, parents receive an educational program that provides vocational and career planning services to motivate them to pursue their identified career and educational goals. The second hour of the day the parents and children are together in a program devoted to development of quality learning habits that can be transferred to the home environment. This second hour is structured to promote the parent as the educator and as an effective role model for her children. The goal is for the children to begin learning at an early age and to promote enrollment into formal early childhood education programs or Head Start. The goal for the parents is to motivate them to pursue literacy, complete their high school education or job training, or seek employment. The third hour can include speakers, vocational counseling, computer literacy classes at the OIC center, or tutoring with literacy volunteers.

Methods and Materials

Carla Fuentes, a mother in the project said, "I have been in the program for four months and it has helped me learn of my inner abilities and strengths. I have since applied for school this fall. I have also found a field of studies that will lead toward a rewarding career. I am very grateful for the opportunity to be part of this program for without it I would more than likely still be in neutral."

A typical week in the My Mom and Me program allows mothers to participate in a variety of activities that develop parenting skills, life skills, and library skills and help them reach personal educational goals. At the learning centers in the OIC, parenting skills are developed as the parent and child work together and a staff member makes suggestions about discipline, child development, problem solving, and daily child-rearing responsibilities. Discussions, handouts, and activities are used to reinforce the skills that are introduced. Developing life skills, such as budgeting, as well as information on banking, housing, career opportunities, community agency purposes, and obtaining a driver's permit are addressed through group discussions, exercises, handouts, tours, and individual lessons. Participants are involved daily in group discussions and given workshop materials on family issues, children, school, and career. Speakers from the community address issues on co-dependency, abuse, stress, health issues, and personal care.

Representatives from various careers speak about the necessary training, opportunities, and challenges in specific fields. Many participants are currently involved in individual study using several different pre-GED texts. They submit individual lessons for correction and can then gauge how they have progressed in preparation for the GED test.

Library skills are being developed through the Learn to Read program developed by the West Virginia Library Commission. Mothers complete a lesson worksheet and work with a literacy volunteer. The participants are also using remedial software.

Each Tuesday, mothers and children attend storytime with the children's librarian, who reads several books. The mothers and children then do a project together. Also each week, mothers read to their children and to each other, as well as go to the library to do assignments or spend some time with the librarian learning about different materials and services at the library.

The library staff provide training for parents in the My Mom and Me program who want to volunteer as aides during the children's storyhour. This opportunity gives parents a chance to participate as positive role models for their children, helps to build their confidence, and encourages reading-related activities that can be duplicated in the home.

A monthly award incentive program gets participants involved in their parenting, reading, library skills, academics, and life skills. For each incentive achieved an award (a coupon for free videos or personal time at the library while your child is cared for by the staff, a chance to spend the day observing someone working in the field of your choice, or lunch at a local restaurant) is given. The community has been generous in providing these.

Personnel

Cheryl Kuykendall is the project team coordinator of My Mom and Me. Other team members include Lois Thompson, Marion County Library, and Lynette Orbivich and Thelma Ford from the North Central (WV) Opportunities Industrialization Center, Inc.

Recruitment and Cooperating Agencies

Many agencies assisted the project by providing in-kind resources, referrals, and staff. Cooperating agencies include the Fairmont Housing Authority; Head Start; Literacy Volunteers of Marion County, the Board of Education's Adult Education Department; Department of Human Services; the Marion County Health Department; Hope Incorporated (domestic violence shelter) and Fairmont State College.

Staff from My Mom and Me use some creative ways to reach parents and encourage them to participate in the program. They work with the Housing Authority and offer a Section 8 voucher for subsidized housing to families that join the program.

Door-to-door recruiting is a very effective recruitment method. The pre-school teacher and the project coordinator visit the homes of potential participants. This assists the teacher in understanding the child's environment and assessing the home relationship of mother and child.

Transportation to the project site is critical in a rural area and very important as a recruitment tool. Child care for younger and older siblings is also offered to minimize barriers to participation. The staff also receives referrals from Head Start and the cooperating agencies mentioned above. Public service announcements are sent to radio and television stations, and notices are placed in food subsidy baskets on distribution days. Many program participants are recruited by word of mouth.

Project coordinators and other professional staff were recruited through newspaper advertisements. A teacher's aide was recruited from the first group of successful program graduates, and volunteers were recruited from the Fairmont State College School of Education and Child Development and from community social and civic organizations.

My Mom and Me was successful in maintaining 80 percent retention of the program participants. All parents who completed the program have gone on to community adult education programs, obtaining job training or employment.

Costs

Pre-school aide	$ 374.00
Bookkeeper	150.00
Brochures	85.50
Supplies	150.00
Books, records	1,590.00
AV materials	200.00
Transportation	1,500.00
Total	$4,049.50

Support Services

The Health Department provides early childhood screening services and preventive health care education. Literacy Volunteers of Marion County provides tutors for adults.

Special Services

Participants in My Mom and Me needing counseling to deal with issues such as alcoholism, spousal abuse, or other problems were referred to community social agencies.

Grow Your Own Readers

Rockbridge Regional Library
138 South Main St.
Lexington, VA 24450
Contact: Elaine Bezanson
(703) 463-4324

Rockbridge Regional Library and Literacy Volunteers of America of the Rockbridge Area (LVRA) teamed up to create "Grow Your Own Readers." The focus is on developing parenting skills and increasing communication between parents and their children. Other participating community agencies include the Department of Social Services, Adult Basic Education of Rockbridge County, and the city and county school districts.

Within the program framework, storytelling became a successful way to get adults into reading-related activities. Parents were encouraged to participate in storytime activities with their children and to tell stories from their childhood, skills that do not require knowing how to read. Parents were also shown how to make and use puppets and flannel boards to tell stories. Wordless books, concept books, and predictable story books were all used to help parents learn to enjoy spending time with their children.

Telling stories about their own families encouraged parents to begin building a sense of family tradition and also created a shared learning experience between parent and child. Parents experienced a positive way to interact with their children which encouraged them to continue reading-related activities at home.

You Are a Teacher Because You Are a Parent is a booklet created by the project team coordinator and given to all parents who participated in the program. Inside, there are many suggestions for parents to help their children develop listening skills; vocabulary and language development; alphabet concepts, words, visual discrimination; number concepts; shapes; colors; and sequences. In addition, all families were provided with children's books, take-home craft projects, and low-vocabulary handouts.

This project helped bring several community agencies together and the library was the coalescing agency. As project team coordinator, Elaine Bezanson, said, "In times when private and public funding is tight, agencies need to avoid duplication of services and need to search for creative ways of working together to serve the same target families. The Grow Your Own Readers project made agency administrators begin to think about interagency cooperation."

Description and Approach

Rockbridge Regional Library and four branch libraries serve a predominately rural population of 36,000 in Rockbridge County and parts of Bath County. Lexington and Buena Vista are the largest cities with populations of about 7,500 each. A bookmobile travels to the smaller, more remote areas of these two counties. The objective during the grant period was to start small and gradually build a strong program.

Grow Your Own Readers adopted an interactive workshop format to reach the target population, low-literate adults and teenage parents with children up to age 7. Six workshops were offered at two different times, Thursday evenings or Saturday mornings. The themes included Growing Things; Bedtime Stories & Read-Aloud Tips; Halloween Party & Storytelling; Concepts Storytime & First Teachers; Feelings Storytime & Creative Dramatics; and Teddy Bear's Picnic with Poetry.

Each two-hour workshop consisted of a theme storytime attended by all family members, a parent time to help adults develop positive parenting skills while children participated in story-related craft activities and a time when parents and children worked together to share their new skills. Several storybook characters came to the workshops and each shared his or her adventures with the families.

Volunteers greeted parents as they entered the room and before the program began, each volunteer introduced a parent to the group. This creative way to "break the ice" helped parents get to know one another and to relax and enjoy the program.

Methods and Materials

Each interactive two-hour workshop featured a theme storytime attended by all family members, a parent time, a children's activity time, and a time when parents and children worked together. Kits to take home that reinforce the concepts also helped parents to continue the learning. Books, craft kits, book lists, and storytime scripts were given to each family at each workshop. Cassette tapes of the storytimes and copies of video tapes were provided to several families. Following is an outline for the Bedtime Stories and Read-Aloud tips workshop. Other workshops followed a similar format.

A. "Good Night, Sleep Tight" Storytime

Adults and children sit together and are encouraged to participate in all activities. The leader models positive interaction with children for the parents, as well as a love of stories and books.

1. Books read or told include: Bonsall's *Who's Afraid of the Dark;* Stoddard's *Bedtime for Bear;* Wood's *The Napping House;* Baum's *I Want to See the Moon.*
2. Dramatics for audience participation include "Getting Ready for Bed"; Five Little Monkeys fingerplay; and The Stars are Twinkling fingerplay.
3. Songs include "Rock-a-Bye Baby"; "Twinkle, Twinkle, Little Star"; and "There Were Ten in the Bed."
4. Magic trick performed was "Dolls in the Cradle."

B. Children's Activity Time: Night Sky and Rhyming Words

A child care aide and babysitters direct activities for children to reinforce the storytime concepts and reading readiness.

1. Glow-in-the-Dark night sky pictures were created using dark blue construction paper, chalk, glow-in-the-dark stars, and glow-in-the-dark paint.
2. Children watch their creations sparkle and glow in the dark room.
3. The concept of rhyming words from *Goodnight Moon, Mother Goose,* and *Hop on Pop* is presented to the children.
4. Children enjoy moon-shaped crescent cookies with milk for a snack.

C. Parent Activity Time: Reading Aloud and Sharing Books

A leader directs parents in activities which will encourage them to work with their children at home and engages parents in discussion of common problems.

1. A volunteer and the children's librarian presented an original skit about two young mothers with many children. In the skit, one mother didn't read well and the other mother told her of the importance of sharing books with her children, suggested creative ways to share books without knowing all the words, and directed the non-reading mother to a library-based literacy program.
2. Tips for effective reading aloud by modeling and asking for input on good and bad methods (too fast, monotone, etc.)
3. Modeled reading and practice of book to be given away (Brown's *Goodnight Moon*).
4. Library cards and bibliographies distributed to parents and children.
5. Kit of "Make Your Own Goodnight Book" was distributed followed by a discussion of bedtime rituals.

D. Family Time

The leader helps families to interact with each other in positive ways. Parents and children spend some time together sharing their new book. Each family is given a calendar of family activities to do during the week.

The elements of family literacy, modeling positive parenting behaviors for adults, development of reading readiness or pre-reading skills for children, and time for both parents and children to share their new skills together are all incorporated in this program.

Personnel

Elaine Bezanson, children's librarian at Rockbridge Regional Library is the project team coordinator. Other team members include Joe Egyed, Literacy Volunteers of Rockbridge and Ted Campbell, Adult Basic Education of Rockbridge County.

Recruitment and Cooperating Agencies

First, a list of all service providers who have contact with the target population was developed. Ministers, church groups, Chapter 1 teachers, and elementary school principals and counselors were identified. The project coordinator organized a meeting of community leaders to describe the project and ask for volunteers. All contacts received a packet of information explaining the program. Reminder letters requesting the names of target families and then follow-up phone calls were part of the recruiting strategy. The coordinator attended meetings of the Adult Literacy volunteers to ask for volunteers for Grow Your Own Readers.

An easy-to-read flier was developed and distributed to families through pre-schools, Head Start, ABE, Job Shop, social services, elementary and high school counselors, and adult literacy volunteers.

The Department of Social Services cooperated in the project by distributing children's books remaining from the workshops to needy families at Christmas time.

Costs

Coordinator	$2,900
Consultant services	671
Copies	230
Postage and brochure	188
Instructional materials	215
Crafts and refreshments	200
Books to give away	600
Total	$5,000

In-kind contributions of $1,117 were received from the Rockbridge Regional Library. Total cost of the project was $6,117.

Support Services

The library provides office space for Grow Your Own Readers and office and tutoring space for adult literacy tutoring. The library vigorously supports literacy efforts with family literacy materials and a New Readers collection.

READ TOGETHER

Carnegie Library of Pittsburgh
Homewood Branch
Beginning with Books Program
7101 Hamilton Ave.
Pittsburgh, PA 15208

Contact: Susan LeWay
(412) 731-3080

"I feel happy about my reader because she tells me a lot of good stories. . . . For those who don't know, reading is very important these days." The 7-year-old who wrote those words was sharing her feelings about the READ TOGETHER program.

Partners in this family literacy project were the Greater Pittsburgh Literacy Council and Beginning with Books, a family literacy agency affiliated with the Carnegie Library of Pittsburgh. The council provides literacy tutors for adults and READ TOGETHER recruits and trains volunteers to read to the children or grandchildren of these adult learners while they attend literacy classes. The one-on-one sessions occur at eight branches of the library.

"D," a very soft-spoken woman with a wonderful sense of achievement, said that because of the READ TOGETHER program, her children were doing well in school; in fact they were ahead of their peers and they loved books and couldn't get enough of the library. She is trying to encourage other friends of hers, also mothers with small children, to get into the program.

Description and Approach

Pittsburgh is a city that has made the transition from heavy industry to a service economy. Many residents have been ill-prepared for this switch, so there is a sizeable population without marketable skills, especially literacy skills. Many dislocated and discouraged workers lack the literacy skills to re-enter the economy, as do many young people just entering the workforce.

Pittsburgh shares with many other urban centers the problems faced by inner-city families: low income, inadequate education, and drug-related violence. For children in these families, there are few models of functioning, satisfying literacy skills and usually no one at home to provide the read-aloud experience so necessary to the development of readers.

The Carnegie Library of Pittsburgh maintains 18 city branches and outreach reading centers in several low-income and public housing communities. READ TOGETHER sites are located in eight of the branch libraries.

READ TOGETHER is a family literacy program founded in 1987 through a United Way grant. It recruits volunteers to read one-on-one to children, usually while their parents are receiving literacy tutoring from the Greater Pittsburgh Literacy Council. The sessions provide literacy enrichment for the children and the child care that enables young parents to pursue tutoring. Literacy-related games, art materials, and puzzles are also available when participants need a break in the reading. Each child receives three gift books during the course of the year. Although the children's literacy development and enthusiasm for books have been impressive and the retention rate excellent, one objective of the program—that the parent begin reading to the child as his or her literacy skills improve—has not been realized. The Bell Atlantic/ALA Family Literacy Project grant addressed this need.

Methods and Materials

To achieve the goal of increasing home reading to children, READ TOGETHER developed training and support materials in family literacy for the Greater Pittsburgh Literacy Council (GPLC). Tutors were trained by the Beginning with Books staff and then GPLC used the training module of Beginning with Books to integrate their family literacy approach into GPLC's ongoing training. Four volunteer tutor training sessions were held and a total of 282 literacy tutors were instructed in using children's books as tutoring materials and encouraging home storybook reading. The success of the training has been measured by comparing the number of adult students who indicated on their goals checklist that they wished to read to their children or grandchildren or help them with homework with the number who are actually doing so. Tutors reported that 173 parents say they are now reading to their children at home. The tutor-training module and handouts have also been shared with three other adult literacy providers.

Written materials to encourage parents with limited reading skills to read to their children are another tool used to achieve the goal of more parent participation. A pamphlet, with tips on reading to children, was rewritten at the third grade reading level. The content remained the same, but the text and individual sentences were shortened and vocabulary was simplified. New photographs added multicultural appeal and increased white space and margins made the pamphlet easier to read. This pamphlet, entitled "Beginning with Books," is distributed to all GPLC tutors, homeless shelters, well baby clinics, and over 35 other agencies serving low income families. Three thousand copies were printed with the grant and Westinghouse donated the printing of 12,000 additional copies. A second pamphlet, "Books to Begin With," was created and lists appealing and easy-to-read children's books.

Because of the READ TOGETHER program every new tutor trained by the Greater Pittsburgh Literacy Council receives training in family literacy and many are supporting parents' efforts to read to their children. The Beginning with Books program offers family literacy training to several adult literacy programs, and the easy-to-read parent pamphlet mentioned above is enclosed in gift book packets that are distributed to many other agencies throughout the city.

Personnel

Susan LeWay is the project team coordinator and Elizabeth Segel and Joan Friedberg are co-directors of Beginning with Books. Other team members include Karen Munde from the Greater Pittsburgh Literacy Council and Paula Cox from Bell of Pennsylvania.
Recruitment and Cooperating Agencies

Volunteer readers are recruited through newspaper and radio announcements. The Volunteer Action Center of the United Way and the coordinator of volunteers at the Carnegie Library both refer participants to the program coordinator. Once interested people contact the office, the program coordinator interviews them by phone and then sends out a job application. Applications are reviewed and volunteers are notified of the next training. Volunteers are asked to make at least a six-month commitment.

Mike Connors, a former member of the project team and volunteer from Bell of Pennsylvania put a notice in the employee newsletter to help recruit volunteer readers. Connors has now transferred to another city and the new Bell of Pennsylvania employee volunteer is Paula Cox, who is involved with READ TOGETHER as a volunteer reader. She also helped raise funds to partially underwrite the annual READ TOGETHER party.

Parents are recruited through referrals from adult literacy training agencies and local social service agencies. Media announcements are successful, but the most effective method is often a participating parent suggesting the program to a relative or friend. The coordinator explains the program to the parent and then matches the child with the most appropriate volunteer reader, being careful to consider factors of time, personality, the child's age, and preferred library site.

Costs

Special Materials	
Activity supplies	$ 600
Volunteer manuals	200
1,000 Book lists	340
3,000 Pamphlets	600
Gift books	900
Consultant Services	
9 Tutor trainings	$ 360
Writing the tutor manual section	200
Drawing up and formatting book lists	600
Rewriting pamphlet for low-literate parent	400
Beginning with Books training	600
Promotion	
2,000 fliers	$ 200
Total	$5,000

In-kind contributions and matching funds totaled $27,450 from these agencies: Carnegie Library; Vista; United Way; Allegheny Conference on Community Development; and the Greater Pittsburgh Literacy Council.

Support Services

The library maintains a Literacy Resource Materials Network to support the work of local literacy instruction providers. The library donates space to the Greater Pittsburgh Literacy Council for a field office/assessment center, for tutoring sessions, and provides delivery of literacy materials to all units. The library has materials for adult new readers from the beginning level to eighth grade. Read-Aloud Parent Clubs, which teach and encourage Head Start parents to read to their children, meet at two branches.

Special Services

Beginning with Books, located at the Carnegie Library's Homewood Branch, has been a primary focus of the library's literacy efforts since 1986. The program's philosophy "that the most effective way to promote literacy is to assist parents and caregivers in providing young children with the critical early experiences that lead to success as readers" continues to be a model for family literacy programs within the national and international arena. Parent education programs use materials developed by Beginning with Books, and its Gift Book Program has been replicated in dozens of communities. Requests for materials have come from 35 states and four countries. Beginning with Books has originated four separate programs: the Gift Book Program; READ TOGETHER; Read-Aloud Parent Clubs; and Project BEACON.

Newport News Public Library

2400 Washington Ave.
Newport News, VA 23607
Contact: Patricia Berry
(804) 247-8677

The Newport News family literacy project was developed with the Peninsula Literacy Council and the Newport News public schools. The program is held in the library and while children enjoy storytime, parents attend literacy classes that focus on developing reading skills that can be used with children and parenting skills that include nutrition information and child-rearing skills.

Project director Patricia Berry redesigned the original project when she realized that it was not developing as effectively as she had originally planned. The project began in June 1990 and by August Berry had decided to make some significant changes in the program. The turning point came during the training workshop which all project grant recipients are required to give to other community agencies.

The training workshop included a panel of resource mothers from the Office of Human Affairs who became a key factor in mobilizing the community agencies into action. They agreed to attend special family literacy training sessions at the library and to encourage teen mothers to read to their children. Together, they learned more about the library-based family literacy program and through collaboration these women and representatives from other agencies worked out the original problems and came up with solutions that ultimately strengthened the program. The Chesapeake and Potomac (C&P) Telephone of Virginia employee volunteer, Barbara James, became very involved with the project. She organized a children's book and magazine drive. Although her office is located in Richneck in the northern part of the city, she and six of her staff all became trained tutors. The workshop's keynote address was delivered by the city's adult education assistant director who discussed the causes and consequences of low literacy in Newport News.

The most gratifying aspect of the family literacy program, according to Patricia Berry,

> is that the Newport News Family Literacy Program has changed, in positive ways, the lives of all who have become involved with it. We convinced one of our students who has excellent artistic ability that she was good enough to have a market for her work. She reluctantly agreed to illustrate a manual for a local company. Her reading ability seemed to blossom simultaneously with her new self-confidence. After less than a year in the program she has entered the local community college and is taking her first course towards an associate's degree in commercial art. She still comes to her tutor when she needs help. She is more productive on her job as a meat packer in a local company, knowing that she will not have to do that for the rest of her life.

Description and Approach

This family literacy program was developed with the Peninsula Literacy Council and focuses on helping parents and other adult caregivers to acquire skills necessary for teaching reading readiness to their preschool children. The program provides both individual and shared learning opportunities for parents and children and gives parents an opportunity to interact with other parents. Parents attend literacy classes and also receive instruction on parenting skills, nutrition information, and child-rearing skills through the cooperation of the Adult Basic Education Department of the public schools.

The family literacy program is located in a branch library in the area of the city with the lowest income level, most single parent households, and lowest education level. In Newport News, approximately 6,900 families are female, single, and head of household. The percent of those 25 years of age and over with less than a ninth grade education is 16 percent or 12,860 persons. State statistics indicate that the combined efforts of both the public and private sectors are reaching only an estimated 2.8 percent of the population in need. The target audience for this family literacy project is single parent families, especially families headed by teenage mothers who have not completed high school.

The classes are developed in cooperation with social services and the Adult Basic Education Department of the public schools. The Peninsula Literacy Council assists with tutor training and matching tutors with parents. The Adult Basic Education program accepts family literacy participants who read at or above the fifth grade level. Those who test at fourth grade level and below receive instruction at the library.

Methods and Materials

This project changed significantly from the original proposal. Initially, it was structured as six-week sessions designed around a theme and offered at specific times. The project changed because parents who wanted to participate needed different accommodations for their school age children. More flexible hours were added to the program and open enrollment allowed parents to get involved with the program at any time during the year.

A gift books component was added to the program and is having a very positive impact. It is based on the model of the "Read to Me" Gift Book Project that is an early intervention gift book program designed to reach low income or low literate families unaware of the benefits of reading at home, owning appropriate children's books, or using the public library. Targeted families are reached through designated agencies, such as public health clinics, homeless shelters, and teen parenting services. Staff members of these agencies speak individually with parents about the importance of reading to their children and then give parents the gift book packets. Each family enrolled in the program receives a packet containing a children's book, a coupon for an additional free book, which is redeemable upon completing an entire session of the family literacy program, a bookmark, and an easy-to-read pamphlet explaining how to make reading a part of daily family activities.

Recruitment and Cooperating Agencies

Recruitment has been a challenge from the beginning of this project and recruitment methods have also been modified from the original proposal. The project started by relying on referrals from other agencies, but staff in the agencies did not have a clear understanding of the family literacy project and how it could help families. To address this important issue, Patricia Berry developed the training workshop to train public health nurses, homeless shelter directors, and instructors of teen parenting classes how to explain the importance of parents reading to their children, how to use the gift books program, and how to follow up by enrolling clients in the family literacy program. Each agency is asked to identify staff members who are responsible for carrying out the reading recommendations to parents. Agencies have pledged among themselves to work more closely with families to strengthen the reading commitment.

Retention was also a problem initially, but the rate increased among participants when specially trained resource mothers encouraged their peers to stay in the program. More flexible hours were added to the program to accommodate parents who wanted to participate:

Costs

Books for library collection	$2,265
Gift books for participants	2,264
Workshop meals	160
Total	$4,689

In-kind contributions of personnel and services were received from the library, the Peninsula Literacy Council, the Adult Basic Education Department of the Newport News public schools, and local printers, amounting to $7,691. Total cost of the project was $12,380.

Support Services

The library system maintains a collection of over 350 items for adult basic education and there are over 1,400 items in the branch library (project site) that include literacy tutoring materials and easy reader materials for those with low reading skills. The library system has also purchased a computer and literacy software which can be used by individual students or with a tutor. The annual book budget is approximately $2,000 for the purchase of literacy-based materials, and additional funds are donated by the Friends of the Library. Approximately 2 percent of the library's materials budget is used for literacy and ABE materials.

Special Services

Parents in the program who have older children receive help from the staff with school-related items. Sometimes they need help reading school-generated communications dealing with parent/teacher conferences, deciphering home assignments, etc. Staff of the family literacy project are now currently working with the local school district to encourage clearer and simpler writing for parents.

LIFT
Literacy Involves Families Working Together

Cabell County Public Library
455 Ninth Street Plaza
Huntington, WV 25701
Contact: Sally Adkins and Mary Robson
(304) 523-9451

In Huntington, West Virginia, the Tri-State Literacy Council and the Cabell County Public Library developed a program that teaches parents the importance of reading to children and of encouraging the development of their children's cognitive skills to increase chances of success in school.

To introduce the project to the community, a media luncheon was sponsored by Larry Legge, the Bell Atlantic employee volunteer. Local radio and television personnel were invited to the library to hear representatives from community agencies explain the project and talk about family literacy.

The literacy program is called Project LIFT (Literacy Involves Families Working Together) and many agencies in the community are working together to develop this comprehensive lecture and activity series for parents. Two series of workshops are offered. Workshop I is a one-hour reading seminar for Head Start parents presented at each Parent Child Center in Cabell, Lincoln, and Wayne counties. It is presented simultaneously with Workshop II, which is an eight-session series for 12 Head Start parents. Workshop I focuses on learning activities that children need to practice at their particular stage of development. Each parent is given a learning kit containing a toy, a book, and instructions for an activity.

At each Parent Child Center, the director worked with the family literacy project team and the Head Start staff to arrange convenient dates, times, and places for the workshops. The center director also furnished the project team with a list of parents and the ages and names of their children so the team could prepare the learning kit for each child with the appropriate materials in it. The team also purchased a cassette tape recorder for each center so parents could check it out to take home and play the read-along tape furnished by the project team. The parents share ideas about reading with their children, identify ways of helping their children learn, learn to select good books to read with their children, visit the library, get a library card, and learn about reading-related activities they can do with their children. These Head Start parents meet guest speakers from different community organizations (a faculty member from Marshall University, a school district reading supervisor, book store manager, and others) and they talk to one another.

Joyce is a parent enrolled in the LIFT program. Her young son is enrolled in Head Start and that is how Joyce found out about the family literacy project. She said, "Before I got into this program, the only things in my life were going to the grocery store, doing the laundry, and taking my child to school. I knew there had to be more to life, but I didn't know what."

Through LIFT Joyce became aware of the many choices she has to help herself and her family. With pride and much happiness, Joyce said, "I read to my son just about every day. We talk about what we have read. I also let him pick out the books he wants to read. I know now that when you read to a child, just by the way you read and express yourself, you shape the feelings and emotions of the child."

Description and Approach

Cabell County Public Library is located in Huntington, West Virginia and serves both rural and urban areas. Cabell County has 28,000 adults with less than 12 years of school and 14,000 with less than eight. Project LIFT offers an eight-session series of workshops to (1) encourage parents to share reading with their children; (2) show parents reading-related activities they can do with their children; (3) encourage parents to visit the library and develop a relationship with the children's librarian; and (4) provide a positive experience for parents so they can share a positive experience with their children, i.e., raise the self-confidence level of the parents. Cabell County Public Library and the Tri-State Literacy Council coordinate all the activities and arrange for speakers. The workshops include topics such as the importance of parents to learning; the importance of reading; "getting into" good books; and visiting the library.

Methods and Materials

The project emphasizes the development of parenting skills among a small group of Head Start parents. The workshops are designed to present information to parents from a variety of sources that reinforce the tremendous influence that parents have in the lives of their children. Speakers are invited because of their expertise in areas of child development, children's literature, and related topics. The series emphasizes activities that are part of family life when parents and children are engaged together in positive experiences that can be both enjoyable and educational. Parents are encouraged to talk each week about their children. This arrangement provides an opportunity for parents to give immediate feedback to the project team, who check out how parents were using the information they received in workshops. Parents can also interact with each other and ask questions.

Interaction is an important aspect of the program because many parents with low reading skills live in a somewhat self-imposed isolation and do not interact with their peer group on a regular basis. This setting provides an opportunity for them to discuss interaction with their children, and it also encourages them to continue seeking child development information as well as receiving positive feedback for participation in the program.

Personnel

The project team included Sally Adkins and Mary Robson from Tri-State Literacy Council, Mary Jane Bevins, Southwestern Community Action Council, Susan Ferrell from Marshall University, and Larry Legge, Supervisor, Construction Control, C&P Telephone.

Recruitment and Cooperating Agencies

Parents who participate in the second workshop of the project are recruited by the Head Start staff using family service workers. These Head Start staff members interview parents one-on-one to determine if they are interested in participating in the program. At least one parent from each Head Start center in Cabell County attends the eight-week series. Parents are offered the opportunity to participate and make the choice without knowing there is a stipend for attendance.

In addition to the many agencies listed above who participate in the workshop series, other cooperating agencies included: Cabell County Board of Education, Harts Volunteer Fire Department, and the U.S. Army Corps of Engineers. The Cabell County Library has taken a strong leadership role in the provision of literacy services in West Virginia for many years. When the current library was built, over 10 years ago, an adult literacy classroom and office area were included in the building plans. The library developed and maintains an Information and Referral (I & R) service that is staffed by employees of the Department of Social Services. Many people requiring assistance with housing, food, or other social services use the I & R and the location in the library ensures that literacy services are conveniently offered in the same place where applications for food stamps must be processed. The arrangement has been very successful and has helped people think of the library as a "full service" center for many needs of all age and income groups.

Throughout the project, the Bell Atlantic employee volunteer was supportive and very accessible. This business partner on the family literacy team attended several of the parent workshops and also arranged for participants to meet at the C&P facility and learn some practical aspects about the business of running a phone company.

Costs

100 learning kits @ $10 each	$1,000
Supplies for workshops	300
Bookstore gift certificates	
12 @ $10 each	120
Consultant services	1,000
Promotional materials	300
Transportation costs	500
Parent stipends	
12 @ $15/session x 8	1,440
Total	$4,660

In-kind contributions were received from Cabell County Public Library; Southwestern Community Action Council; Marshall University; Huntington Museum of Art; and Huntington Mall, Waldenbooks and totaled $5,625. Total cost of the project was $10,625.

Support Services

The Cabell County Public Library received an LSCA Title VI grant in April 1987 to begin a new reader's collection. The collection is maintained with 1 percent of the library's annual book budget. Literacy awareness presentations were made at each Head Start parent meeting in Cabell County in the fall of 1989 to lay the groundwork for future literacy involvement by the parents. These awareness presentations were also given to community and civic organizations and the media. Information booths were set up at conferences and seminars; videos and speakers are also available to interested groups. The Tri-State Literacy Council uses more than 100 volunteers annually to serve adult learners in Cabell County.

Special Services

During the project the parents are interviewed individually by staff concerning what goals they have identified for themselves and what they want to accomplish. Through these interviews, parents become aware of the many sources of information and services available to them and referrals to other agencies help the parents begin to take positive steps to achieve their identified goals.

Many parents identified a desire to enroll in the CDL (Commercial Driver's License) program to get the license needed to drive a school bus. Several parents are now working for Head Start as bus drivers and providing transportation to programs throughout the county. Some parents are working to pass the GED and receive a high school diploma, and others have gone into a nurse's aide program at the local community college.

CALIFORNIA'S FAMILIES FOR LITERACY

Families for Literacy (FFL)

Long Beach Public Library and Information Center
101 Pacific Avenue
Long Beach, CA 90802-4482
Contact: Mary Donberg
(213) 437-2949

Long Beach Public Library and Information Center has developed a traditional type of family literacy program modeled on an expanded storytime. Programs are held in the library and at the Tarzana Treatment Center (TTC), a drug/alcohol rehabilitation center for women. Although it is limited to families with at least one pre-school age child, this program targets the families of learners currently enrolled in the library's adult literacy program and recruits new families through TTC and the 12 local Head Start centers.

Mary Donberg, FFL coordinator for the library, offers the following guidelines to other family literacy programs:

1. Be persistent—don't give up on a learner
2. Be flexible—with learners, tutors, and library staff
3. Be creative and be brave—don't be afraid to try new things
4. Listen and respond to learner needs

One success story from the Long Beach program involves a young man and his pregnant wife. Donberg tried to get this couple to attend one of her literacy sessions for the entire time the wife was pregnant, but the couple saw no need to attend since they did not yet have a child. After the child was born, Donberg continued to urge them to attend with their baby, but the parents felt the child was too young to participate.

Finally, when the baby was 8 months old, the parents agreed to attend a special Christmas storytime. After the program, Donberg realized that the baby had not responded (being too far from the book and the reader to maintain interest), and she quickly asked if she could hold the baby. She sat down with a few board books featuring brightly colored pictures and began to read. The baby was attentive and responded by cooing and reaching for the books. The parents were amazed (how smart their baby must be to respond at so young an age) and convinced. They have attended every program session since.

Another highlight of the Long Beach family literacy program has been the participation of one special family and its eight children. Both parents were so delighted with the program that they agreed to speak about it to the Long Beach City Council at a budget hearing. Their comments were so effective and moving that the Council agreed to fund the coordinator and a support staff position with city funds. The minimal state grant now needed by the library is used primarily to purchase books for the book giveaway program and instructional materials for the families.

Description and Approach

Long Beach Public Library, with a main library and 11 branches, serves the city of Long Beach, which is located on the coast of southern California south of Los Angeles. The ethnic makeup of this community of 415,000 has become increasingly diverse over the last decade. What was once a primarily white, middle class community is now almost 50 percent minority. The minority population is predominantly Hispanic, but it also includes Asian, African American, and American Indian ethnic groups. The community is also diverse in socioeconomic terms, containing pockets of poverty as well as areas of wealth.

From the beginning, the family literacy program involved the library's Youth Services Department and the staff of Project Read, the adult component of the library's literacy services. All of the children's librarians have given their support to the project, hosting storytimes and special family sessions, compiling book lists as needed, and giving special welcomes to families visiting the library.

Tutors are important to the program. They receive an orientation at each tutor training session and the coordinator also works with individual learner-tutor pairs to show them how children's books can be used in the learner's curriculum.

Methods and Materials

The Long Beach program provides four to six annual series of four storytime sessions for eligible families. The usual format is to serve refreshments first (this allows latecomers to arrive without interrupting the session and also encourages participants to be on time). The entire family then enjoys a traditional library storytime in an adjacent room. After the storytime and related songs, games, fingerplays, and puppetry, the adults remain in the room and participate in a variety of activities that deal with parenting, improving their own reading and writing skills, and addressing the emerging literacy needs of their children.

The coordinator and tutors work with the parents on topics that include learning through play and language and speech development. Much of the instruction parents receive about reading aloud to their children occurs as they see the librarian sharing books when the entire family is together. In the separate parent meeting later, the librarian further discusses techniques of book sharing. Gift books presented to the children are always read aloud to the parents, and any aspects of the story which may stimulate discussion or observations by the child are stressed. A special point is made of the relationship of the illustration to the text.

Parents also receive general tips about creating a reading environment free of distractions and providing a comfortable and special spot for reading. A strong emphasis is placed on making reading aloud to the child a warm, nurturing, natural activity.

Knowing that the concept of family reading may be entirely new to these parents, the coordinator and tutors prepare them to deal with common situations such as a child not paying attention to the story, frequent interruptions by the child, or the parent's own boredom in reading a title the child wants to hear again and again. Parents are encouraged to expand the storytelling and storyreading experience by using flannel board stories, homemade books, dramatizations, and original storytelling using wordless picture books and stories from their own experiences.

While parents are occupied, the children continue to hear stories, make related craft objects, or see movies about a story they have just heard. The primary difference between the family literacy program storytime and a typical library storytime is that the children vary in age from infancy to early teens and the parents or primary caregivers are also participating.

Although some of the children's librarians were originally apprehensive about working with such a mixed group, they found that children of all ages were eager to participate. Because the older children and the parents have themselves never been read to or exposed to quality children's books, they seem to enjoy the storytimes as much as the younger children. The older children are very helpful with the younger children and with organizing the props that go along with the stories.

The state grant requires that each program provide gift books for the children. At Long Beach, families are given books when they attend an FFL program or a Project Read event. Books are also distributed to learners when the coordinator meets with the learner/tutor team to conduct book talks and orientation. In addition, books are distributed to families as rewards for meeting their reading goal of a certain number of reading sessions per month. The library is always promoted as the primary resource for children's books.

Recruitment and Cooperating Agencies

Recruitment of families which have one parent or primary caregiver already enrolled in Project Read has been time-consuming but effective. The library uses frequent and consistent mail and telephone contact to encourage parent attendance at programs. At this point, many adult learners have not yet been matched with tutors, so the family literacy program is their first introduction to library programs. Once tutors are assigned, their support is also enlisted in encouraging attendance.

When parents and children benefit from attendance at special programs, they tend to return. In fact, parents often bond together to form informal support networks. Sending party invitations to the children has been very successful in getting families to the library.

Recruitment beyond the Project Read group of learners has been more difficult. The coordinator has made special presentations to the Head Start center, Family Shelter for the Homeless, Long Beach School for Adults, Long Beach Naval Station, and other facilities. The children's librarians talk to children about family literacy during school visits and encourage them to take information home to their parents. The coordinator has trained all children's librarians to be sensitive to the needs of adult learners. As a direct result of the school visits, a number of parents were successfully referred to Project Read.

One very effective recruitment strategy implemented recently was the promotional theme, "Give a Gift to Yourself, Give a Gift to Your Child," which attracted five to ten new families to Project Read. The promotion pointed out the many benefits of adult literacy and offered a sign-up bonus to all new learners with children under 5 consisting of three outstanding titles—*Chicka Chicka Boom Boom, Where's Spot?*

and a *Wee Sing* cassette tape and book. The gift books are highly effective in retaining families in the program as well as being excellent recruitment incentives.

Costs

	State	City
Part-time FFL coordinator and part-time support staff		$48,754
Gift books	$3,000	
Library materials		300
Office supplies		200
Instructional resources (includes refreshments)	1,300	
Contract services	500	
Printing	750	250
Other	100	500
Indirect	307	(2,726)
Total	$5,957	$52,730

In-kind contributions of personnel and services were received from the library, especially from the Youth Services staff. Rancho Los Alamitos was also a partner in fund-raising and promotion.

Support Services

The library provides literacy instruction for adults through its Project Read program. It maintains a large collection of new reader materials and supplies training and administrative services for volunteers who offer one-on-one tutoring for adults. In addition the library has established an After-School Study Center (ASSC), which provides tutoring and other school-related assistance to youth attending school. Older children of FFL families in need of this type of help are referred to the study center. Some family storytimes have been conducted at the same time and location as the after-school program, allowing the older children to work with an ASSC tutor while the parents and younger siblings participate in the storytimes.

Special Services

To assist learners in selecting books for their children a number of book lists are provided for both preschoolers and school age children. Parents also receive a brief tour of the children's section of the library that highlights the picture book and easy book sections. Tutors assist parents in the library as part of their regular tutoring responsibilities.

The coordinator gives a bibliography of family life materials appropriate for Project Read learners to the tutor, who then assists the learner with book selection. In addition, a book display of library items related to the topics discussed is present at all special programs. Items from the library's extensive video collection are included in the display.

Patterns for Reading

National City Public Library
200 East 12th St.
National City, CA 92050-3399
Contact: Beverly Whitcomb or Russ Hamm
(619) 474-2142

National City Public Library has had a Families for Literacy (FFL) program since 1988. The program was originally called PATterns for Reading because the library worked so closely with the National City School District's Department of Early Childhood Education and its PAT (Parents as Teachers) program. Eventually the capital letters were dropped from the first word; the library's program is now called simply "Patterns for Reading."

Patterns for Reading, an extension of the library's successful adult literacy program Project Read, works with families of adult learners from the library's own program as well as with PAT families, GAIN (Greater Avenues for Independence) families, the local Teen Mom Program and "Project New Chance." (GAIN works with parents receiving government aid for dependent children to help them gain greater economic independence.)

PAT is designed to foster maximum parenting skills and to help parents become involved in early learning. Trained parent educators make monthly home visits and provide instruction, behavior modeling, and information about child growth and development. One of the PAT messages to young parents is "Read to your baby from the time you get home from the hospital."

Patterns for Reading provides a remarkable series of 16 carefully developed special family literacy programs that are presented by the FFL coordinator twice each month from November through June.

Scheduling the program on two weekday mornings and one evening each month increases participation by fathers. Each session has a special topic, focus, and printed materials. Every family entering the conference rooms receives the same one or two books along with other handouts, including the session's new pages of poems and songs. These materials are inserted in a three-ring binder which each family receives at the first session. Attendance is steady because the families do not want to miss out on a new section for their "book."

The special sessions include topics such as: library services; becoming acquainted with the children's library; reasons to read to your child; choosing books for your child; wordless picture books and books for a short attention span; concept books; books on parenting; and language skills through children's books.

Description and Approach

National City Library is a branch library located in the South Bay of San Diego County, approximately 10 miles from the border with Mexico. National City has the highest unemployment rate, the lowest household income, the youngest median age, and the highest percentage of ethnic minorities of all the cities in San Diego county. Latinos are the predominant ethnic population. The educational level of National City residents is also one of the lowest in the county: 39 percent of those over age 18 do not complete high school. The city's population is highly transient, with people from Mexico moving into the community daily. When they find jobs or save enough money, they move to other locations in the state.

Methods and Materials

Each of the coordinator's morning programs lasts one hour and covers one topic, while the evening programs last one and one-half hours and cover two topics. The program begins with a session involving parent-child activities that usually lasts about 20 minutes: parents are encouraged to join their children on the floor or hold them on their laps during this time. The coordinator has found that this approach works best because the children are fresh and their attention span is longer at the beginning of the program.

Families have a special binder to which pages are added at each session. Page numbers from the binders are brought to parents' attention during the various activities to help them follow the written word while the coordinator leads the children. Songs, poems, finger plays and flannel board stories and rhymes inserted in the binders are printed on colored paper corresponding with the color of the top strip on the easel board at each session. The color coding helps parents to sort and find materials easily.

During the second part of each program parents go to an adjoining room while children work on a craft project with aides. At this time parents receive information on topics related to parenting and literacy development, often from staff members of the National City School District. The materials and topics selected for these presentations reflect the diverse ethnic makeup of the community.

At the end of each program refreshments are served and a drawing is held for door prizes, which are always books or props related to the topic of the stories read that day. Everyone eagerly looks forward to this part of the program and it is an additional incentive to get families to come back.

The free books that are part of every Patterns for Reading program appeal to the families as much as the poems and song pages they receive for their binders. Families receive more than 160 poems, rhymes, and songs during the 16 sessions, and more than $200 worth of books each year.

One important impact of the program is that adult learners are introduced to the rich world of children's literature; these materials then become part of their own reading skills development. Patterns for Reading makes a point of emphasizing library resources. Adult learners may previously have seen the library as merely a site where they received tutoring, but they now see it as a source of materials. Since adult learners are involved with helping their children, they can confidently seek materials in the children's collections without embarrassment. This opens up a wealth of quality literature which they can handle even if their reading levels are low.

Recruitment and Cooperating Agencies

The target audience for Patterns for Reading is eligible families in the library's service area; the second key target group is PAT families. The program also works with three other community partners. GAIN

(Greater Avenues for Independence), a county program for parents of small children who are undereducated and have poor or marginal employability, attempts to get parents off welfare and into productive jobs. GAIN parents attend a presentation given by the Patterns for Reading coordinator and the Project Read coordinator. They receive an hour's training emphasizing the role of the parent in the literacy and emerging literacy development of their children, and a packet of materials to take home. Even though many of these parents never enroll in Patterns or in Project Read, in this one session they receive enough basic information to help them understand what they should do to make a difference in the development of their young children.

Patterns also works with "Project New Chance," a national demonstration project of Sweetwater Adult School that targets teenage parents who are high school dropouts and on welfare. In addition, Patterns for Reading does outreach to the Teen Mom programs at Del Rey Adult Center and Sweetwater Adult School.

Costs

Part time staff	$16,486
Contract services	7,440
Office supplies	450
Printing	400
Instructional resources	800
Gift books	3,200
Other	240
Total	$29,016

In-kind contributions of personnel and services are received from the library, the Sweetwater Adult School, and the National City School District.

Support Services

Project Read provides ongoing tutoring services to adults in National City and maintains a large collection of new reader materials and tapes. The library has an extensive video collection as well as many materials and videos in Spanish.

Special Services

Each year Project Read and Patterns for Reading present a Chili Cook-Off. In past years many families left the cook-off after receiving their free book, but additional children's activities have resulted in families staying to enjoy musical entertainment, sample chili and salsa, and browse at the Friends of the Library book sale.

Families for Literacy (FFL)

Santa Barbara Public Library
40 East Anapamu
Santa Barbara, CA 93101
Contact: Ruth Smith, FFL Coordinator/
Ann Zimmerman, CLC Coordinator
(805) 564-5618

Santa Barbara Public Library's Families for Literacy (FFL) program began in 1990 as an extension of an existing adult literacy program. The program provides family literacy services in several ways. Volunteer literacy tutors receive tutor training that includes an extensive overview of the program. Adult learners are then paired with tutors who are interested in working with families. Prior to finalizing the tutor-learner match, each tutor receives a tutor handbook and special training from the program coordinator or the adult literacy coordinator. Periodic group tutor in-service sessions are conducted by literacy staff and by outside experts in related fields.

Books and magazines are distributed monthly to the parents by the tutors or during the special events activities planned by the FFL coordinator. The coordinator also conducts group and individual parenting sessions.

Monthly special events activities at the library generally include a storytime and parenting information on children's growth and development. As an example of seasonal activities, a Halloween party in October featured simple costumes, games, and stories. At another event, four firemen from the city fire department talked about fire safety at home, demonstrated safety techniques for fire prevention, and brought a fire engine on-site for the families to explore firsthand. Following the demonstration, children received art supplies, while parents were asked to talk with their children and to write experience stories with them.

Families were then encouraged to read their stories together for family enjoyment. Each special event ends with a story and the distribution of a book to take home.

This program also works with families of women at La Mirada, the Santa Barbara County Honor Farm (a women's jail), and with families in Transition House, a local homeless shelter. Both of these groups (especially those at the homeless shelter) have proved to be more difficult to work with than other adult learners, but working with them has been both successful and rewarding.

One Saturday nearly a year after the program began at the Honor Farm, Ann Zimmerman, the adult literacy coordinator, observed for the first time two children from different families arriving with books given to them for their mothers to share with them on their weekly visits to the Honor Farm. One toddler had *Five Little Monkeys* firmly in his grip and the other had a recently new, but already well-worn, *Goodnight Moon*. The toddler proudly informed Ann that he "reads" his book every single night because his mother is not there to read it to him.

Description and Approach

Santa Barbara Public Library is an eight-branch system which serves the town of Santa Barbara and the surrounding unincorporated community of approximately 180,000 people, as well as some rural parts of the county. Located 85 miles north of Los Angeles, Santa Barbara was once primarily used by wealthy Los Angelenos as a retreat and second home away from the smog and dense population. In the past two decades it has changed considerably, and is now a very diverse community, both ethnically and socio-economically. This diversity appears to be increasing at a steady rate.

As in most of California's FFL programs, tutors play a key role in the success of Santa Barbara's program. Tutors participate in training sessions, meet with individual adult learners two times per week, attend special events activities with learners and their families, and in some instances carry out special activities with the learners independent of the program. Tutors also read to children during the storytime activities.

Most of the gift books in the program are appropriate for preschoolers and are distributed to the families by the tutors. Tutors are expected to devote a 15 to 20 minute portion of each learning session to modeling appropriate reading techniques for parents to use at home. When adult learners feel comfortable reading a book, the book is taken home to be shared with their children and to become a part of the family's library for continuous reading and enjoyment.

To promote the joy of reading, the coordinator periodically takes a box of selected giveaway books to the storytime at the Honor Farm and allows every child to select a book, including those children whose mothers are not part of the FFL program. The giveaway books are children's books that have been in the library collection or have been donated by the public. They are carefully selected according to the guidelines and goals of the program and are appropriate for the developmental ages of the participating children.

Methods and Materials

Although the regular library literacy program families are served through their tutors and through special events generally held at the library, the program for the Honor Farm is structured quite differently. Because these women see their children only on Sundays and the visits are limited to two hours each, parenting and training programs for them are given during the week when the children are not present (topics are the same as those used in the regular literacy program). A special storytime is presented by the FFL or adult literacy coordinator once each month during visitation. It was felt that one time per month would be adequate and would not interfere with the women's limited private time with their families.

Children's books are distributed by the tutor to the participating Honor Farm women during their regular weekly tutoring sessions. A new book is distributed each week, and the women share the book with their children during visitation hours every Saturday. Storytime has provided structure for the families and it has also created excitement and enthusiasm for reading among the children.

Providing family literacy services at Transition House has been a challenge for Santa Barbara's Families for Literacy program. Transition House tries to provide a stable living environment for homeless families for a period ranging from six months to one year. Here, families are already coping with the difficult issues of finding food, shelter, clothing, jobs, and stable schooling; attending to the literacy needs of either parents or children seems more a luxury than a necessity.

Transition House literacy program participants are encouraged to attend the special events which are planned for the program, but special care and attention are required to assure that the families do attend. For example, careful arrangements must be made for transportation. There is a high turnover in this population and many families drop out of the program without giving notice. Finding tutors for this population is very difficult, since tutors must be willing to patiently accept families' failures to show up and other inevitable disappointments. It has also become clear that if the tutor is not able to attend, the chances are that the family will not attend. However, the rewards are so great when the program does work, and the needs are so strong in all of these families, that the library's literacy staff feel it is definitely worth the extra effort needed to serve this population.

Recruitment and Cooperating Agencies

In addition to Transition House and the Honor Farm, the Santa Barbara program recruits from a variety of community partners for its families. GAIN (Greater Avenues for Independence), Casa Rosa and Casa Serena (drug and alcohol recovery homes), Catholic Charities, La Cuesta (a continuation high school), the local Head Start program, and a variety of local churches have proven to be fertile ground for recruitment efforts.

Santa Barbara Public Library has found that frequent and regular meetings with school principals, teachers, parent groups, and community agency directors are necessary in order to maintain referrals for its Families for Literacy program. In addition, brochures and fliers are distributed to hospitals, medical clinics, and selected physicians in the area. Even before the library began its family literacy program, local medical practitioners had developed and distributed a packet for new mothers which included a board book for the newborn and a description of library services for children and families.

The Lompac Public Library and the Santa Barbara Public Library jointly wrote and published a booklet for new parents called "Read— It's Never Too Early to Start." The booklet, which uses photos of a Latino mother and her young infant to help convey its message, can be ordered for a small fee, and a library name and message can be added on the back.

One continuing problem for the Santa Barbara program has been the high mobility rate among families in the area. Also, many community referrals are for adults who can not communicate in English; contacts such as these are referred to local English as a Second Language (ESL) programs for assistance.

Another challenge is the fact that referrals from community agencies generally do not reflect the community's ethnic composition of eligible families as reported in the census data. As a result, the library is now targeting specific agencies to reach under-represented populations, with some degree of success.

The Santa Barbara Kiwanis Club has been a particularly active supporter of the program. They have donated materials for bookcase building among families, conducted a fund-raiser, and sponsored the annual Easter egg hunt. In addition, they have given donations for gift books.

Costs

Part time staff	$14,000
Contract services	700
Travel	500
Office supplies	1,000
Printing	2,000
Instructional resources	3,000
Gift books	8,800
Total	$30,000

In-kind contributions of personnel and services are received from the library. Donations of cash and books are received from a variety of sources and are used to supplement the program budget.

Support Services

The Santa Barbara Public Library's adult literacy program provides ongoing training for volunteers and tutoring for adults at five of the library's eight branches. An extensive collection of new reader materials and videos is maintained by the literacy program and a smaller collection by the library.

New support services are added as needed. One parent who attended parenting sessions at the women's Honor Farm asked for the literacy coordinator to continue the parenting program with her at the next transitional recovery site. The library effort at the new site led to five more eligible parents receiving tutoring and parenting training at that site.

Special Services

Puppets from some children's classics have been purchased for family literacy puppet shows. Volunteers from a local service club act as the characters. These classics are then read at storytimes and copies are given to each family to take home for family reading.

Families for Literacy (FFL)

San Rafael Public Library
1100 E Street
San Rafael, CA 94901
Contact: Jane Iasiello
(415) 485-3318

San Rafael Public Library began its Families for Literacy (FFL) program in 1990 as a component of its library-based adult literacy program. In this tutor-centered FFL delivery system, tutors read children's books aloud in each literacy session with parents. Families are encouraged to attend monthly family storytimes where they select a hardcover book for each child to keep. Once a year children receive a special hardcover birthday book that has been selected with the personality of the child as well as the reading ability of the parent in mind. The program places a high priority on gift books and the building of a home library for families and children.

In their initial training, tutors are given one paperback book for each child in a student's family. The books are selected by the coordinator according to the assessed reading level of the adult learner and the age of the child. This process demonstrates the criteria tutors are to use in selecting books for children in the future. Throughout the year, tutors select one paperback per child per family every month, sometimes with the help of the coordinator, but frequently on their own.

Jane Iasiello, San Rafael's FFL coordinator, places a high priority on her personal involvement with each tutor/learner pair and family, often meeting with the pair during tutoring to give them additional information. One tutor who had not yet received special training reported that it was difficult to tutor a mother when two young children competed for her attention.

Iasiello accompanied the tutor to one literacy lesson, bringing children's books from the library and some colored shapes for sorting. The additional interaction, especially with Iasiello reading stories aloud to the children, was a huge success. Since then and after special training, the tutor has reported that the adult learner reads children's books aloud with the tutor and to her children when they are present, and the pre-literacy materials engage and satisfy the children. With direction from the coordinator, this tutor's problems were resolved and transformed into a positive experience that moved the literacy relationship forward.

Description and Approach

San Rafael is a community of 65,000 located in the heart of Marin County just across the Golden Gate Bridge from San Francisco. The community is becoming more diverse, with the wealthy and upper middle class population being augmented by a growing number of immigrants from Latin America and Southeast Asia who work primarily in service industries. The retired elderly are now sharing the city with more and younger families from other cultures. The San Rafael Public Library is a single branch library.

The library's literacy program serves the entire city. Many adult learners are from the Canal Area, a low-income community with minority populations of African Americans, Hispanic-Americans, and Asian-Americans. The library's strong program of children's services includes monthly storytimes by the children's librarian at local Head Start classes, pre-schools and other child care programs.

Since both the literacy program and the children's department already focused on the Head Start children and their parents for many library services, it seemed natural that the Families for Literacy program should strengthen these cooperative relationships by developing a comprehensive approach to encouraging reading in the home and using the library. Although recruitment of parents from Head Start families into the program has been successful, the library discovered early that using literacy classes to fulfill a Head Start parent improvement requirement is not an effective recruitment strategy. Only when parents make their own decision to connect with the literacy program are they likely to remain in the program.

In the fall of 1990 the Marin County Head Start staff assessed its families' needs for improving their English literacy. Parents who needed basic skill improvement were matched with library literacy tutors in two small groups. Initially the groups met for tutoring twice weekly in a room provided by Head Start, but when these facilities proved inadequate, the groups decided to meet in the home of one of the learners that was convenient to all of them. This solution has worked quite well. Taking the basic adult literacy tutoring to where parents are and working in small groups has been helpful in retaining these parents in the program.

Because of the great cultural diversity of the population this program serves, the coordinator decided to provide as much diversity in books and storytimes as possible, an approach that has helped to shape the way the program provides services.

Methods and Materials

Families come to the library one evening each month for a family storytime which is attended by the entire family (spouse, other relatives, children) of the adult learner, the tutor, and the tutor's children. These meetings are designed to engage and entertain the children with a variety of literacy activities.

A typical storytime begins with an action song that includes families and tutors. The song loosens everyone up, creates a sense of fun, and gets the crowd together as a group. The storytime features stories from various children's books told with the help of different media such as flannel boards, and stick, hand or shadow puppets. Between the stories, fingerplays, action rhymes and body plays give the families a chance to change from passive listeners to active participants. After a puppet show finale, the group moves on to simple crafts, refreshments and the selection of hardcover children's books for the families' home libraries.

Many storytimes have an ethnic theme that introduces families to the stories and culture of their own ethnic groups as well as those of other groups. One theme featuring the Latino culture has been very popular since many of the families are Latino. Both children and parents beam as they sing and shout out words in their native Spanish while bilingual performers play various Latin American instruments and tell stories from several Latino cultures.

Another popular ethnic theme for storytime has been Filipino culture. Although none of the families come from the Philippines, some are from Southeast Asia. Students, families, and tutors count to three and repeat the names of foods and animals in Tagalog, and learn some of the customs of a Filipino crowd attending a festival. The equality which comes with learning together helps to break down the boundaries between student and tutor and parent and child. Everyone is fascinated by the stories and the native costumes worn by the Filipino storyteller and parents and children alike seem to appreciate cultural diversity in a way that encourages self-respect and a broader outlook.

However, much of the important program activity occurs outside of the storytimes during the actual tutoring sessions. Tutors welcome and incorporate children into the literacy lesson whenever it is appropriate. Including children is in itself a statement that enhances full family participation. Tutors show adult learners how to share attention by giving it to the children in turn.

Recruitment and Cooperating Agencies

The program's most effective recruitment strategy has been word of mouth. Initial contacts, primarily with Head Start and the day care center, resulted in a steady stream of new enrollees. Careful and thorough matches between tutors and parents contribute to the success of the program and to the unsolicited participants brought into the program by learners.

The library's partnership with Marin Head Start continues to be more successful each year. Head Start parents who indicate they want to improve English literacy skills as a goal on their Family Needs Assessment are given fliers that refer them to the library's literacy program. The clear communication between the Head Start Family Services director and the FFL coordinator led to the development of a careful literacy intake procedure with the student/tutor coordinator from the library's regular adult literacy program. In the next year, the coordinator intends to collaborate with Head Start's education director to develop a tool to track the impact the family literacy program has had on the Head Start children.

Costs

Contract services (includes part-time FFL staff)	$15,100
Travel	500
Office supplies	200
Printing	500
Instructional resources	1,000
Gift books	2,600
Indirect	1,900
Total	$21,800

In addition to the above budget the library provides $700 for children's materials specially designated for this program. In-kind contributions of personnel and services are also received from the library, particularly from the children's librarian.

Support Services

The library provides ongoing training, materials, and administrative support for volunteers who tutor in both the adult literacy program and its family literacy component. A learning lab with computers and many software programs is also available for the exclusive use of the literacy students and their families. The lab is a major component of the delivery system for the adult program and is regularly used by both adult learners and by the family literacy learners and some members of their families.

Books appropriate for FFL families are identified by the coordinator with a "smiley" sticker on their spines, a device that helps tutors and learners select books from the children's room. Parents can also glance through the shelves and quickly select books without feeling overwhelmed. Parents can ask tutors for help if the books prove too difficult for independent reading.

Special Services

The library staff believes that special programs for parents are ineffective unless parents ask directly or indirectly for information or advice on parenting, child care, and other topics. Instead, staff members select a variety of books on these topics and make them available to tutors. The coordinator is also available to consult with tutors on appropriate ways of approaching these issues with parents. During their training, tutors receive a copy of reading and learning tips for parents to share with their learners.

Project Second Chance's Families for Literacy

Contra Costa County Library
1750 Oak Park Blvd.
Pleasant Hill, CA 94523-4497
Contact: Beth Bockser
(510) 646-6358

Contra Costa County Library began its Families for Literacy program (FFL) in 1989 as an extension of its already successful adult literacy program, Project Second Chance (PSC), which tutors more than 300 adult learners each year. Family literacy efforts are directed to the families of adults already in the PSC program. Initially, the library focused on the Pittsburg and San Pablo communities, but because of the demographics of the county and the number of eligible learners in various places, it now targets its family literacy efforts to the Antioch and Concord communities.

Like Long Beach, Contra Costa based its program on an extended version of the traditional storytime offered in the very active children's services division of the library. Family literacy storytimes focus on reading readiness skills. Because many of the adult learners and their families were unable to attend these FFL special storytimes because of their location, and lack of transportation and time, the program provides most of its family literacy activities through tutors.

Because PSC was already involved with other groups in the county and had been instrumental in the creation of the Contra Costa Literacy Alliance, it was natural that the family literacy program also form varied partnerships. They include an extensive program with a number of Girl Scout troops in which the Girl Scouts help with storytimes and are trained to read aloud to Head Start children. PSC also works with the local council of the California Reading Association to provide new mothers and day care providers with information on the importance of early literacy development. It participates in a full family literacy program for Teen Moms at the Pittsburg Adult School, and is also involved in a program about adult illiteracy presented to elementary school classes by adult new readers.

Enthusiasm for this program has been maintained because of the successes of individual adults and their families. Beth Bockser, the family literacy coordinator, tells of one busy single mother who admits she is often tempted to cancel her tutoring sessions because she is too tired or too busy. But when her two-year-old daughter says, "Go to school mommy so we can get more books," it is hard for her not to go.

Miguel, another parent in the program, showed little interest in family literacy only a year ago. His reading ability has improved tremendously in the past year, however, and so has his interest in the family literacy program. He voluntarily signed his son up for a kindergarten reading program and has committed himself to read to his son fifteen minutes every day.

Description and Approaches

Contra Costa County Library is a county-wide library system with 22 branches located about 20 miles east of San Francisco in East Bay. The county is one of great diversity and contains many communities, some with populations as large as 120,000 and others numbering as few as 125 people. It is primarily suburban, with large pockets of rural areas that are mainly agricultural. The area encompasses steel mills in Pittsburg, orchards in Brentwood, and the major cities of Concord and Walnut Creek.

Family literacy services are provided through the library's Project Second Chance. Tutors are trained in family literacy concepts and receive further instruction at 15 to 20 special programs conducted at the site libraries each year.

The coordinator has developed a number of theme-specific storytimes that focus on the early reading readiness of children. For example, one storytime built around the theme of sequencing uses the primary book, *The Very Hungry Caterpillar.* After this and similar books that involve sequencing are read to the families, the children go off to participate in craft activities that reinforce the concept of sequence, supervised by Girl Scouts and some library staff. Children make their own fruit salad, carefully following the same sequence the caterpillar follows in the book.

While the children are working on the crafts and other activities, the coordinator, parents and tutors go to a different area and discuss the skills taught by the books. The importance of books in the emerging literacy needs of the children is stressed. Topics covered in other sessions include colors, numbers, animals, beginning sounds, and self-esteem.

Methods and Materials

In addition to the regular family literacy programs and activities it provides for PSC learners and their families, Contra Costa's program includes a number of other very successful activities, among them a program with the Girl Scouts. The coordinator has trained over 12 Girl Scout troops and their leaders throughout the county in selecting books for children, using the library and children's librarian as resources, and the importance of reading aloud to children, particularly pre-schoolers. Four to five Girl Scouts then go into Head Start centers, accompanied by their leader, and read aloud to small groups of children. The Girl Scouts earn their literacy badges and children who might never be read to are given that experience.

Project Second Chance, Inc., the fund-raising arm of the library's literacy program, has donated funds for gift books for Head Start children, since they do not qualify for the FFL-funded gift book program unless one of their primary caregivers is enrolled in an adult literacy program. This additional private donation makes gift books available to all children. Both the Girl Scouts and the Head Start centers have been pleased with the program.

In addition to their work at the Head Start centers, some of the Girl Scouts take part in the library's special family literacy programs. They aid the children in craft activities and also help serve refreshments and clean up afterwards.

All of California's family literacy programs must provide gift books for children in participating families. Contra Costa has come up with a unique method for doing this. As a family becomes part of the program, the coordinator records the name and age of each child and their birthday. About two weeks before their birthdays, children receive a special birthday card telling them to go to the children's librarian at the local branch library to receive a free birthday book selected especially for them. The name and address of the closest branch is included on the card.

When children arrive at the library, the children's librarian gives them a wrapped book. The fact that the family presents the special birthday card gives the staff a clue that the family is new to reading and possibly new to this library. The children's librarian gives both parent and child a tour of the children's area and makes sure that both have library cards. This method puts good books into the hands of the child and acquaints parent and child with their local branch library and children's librarian without labeling them as family literacy program participants.

Recruitment and Cooperating Agencies

The target population for this program is the eligible families in the service area. Most families are recruited through the tutor and through phone and mail communication from the coordinator. However, the program continues to work with outside agencies.

One very successful recruitment program has been information and referral outreach to local schools, especially elementary schools. First begun at the request of a local principal, this effort now extends to many schools in the county.

In this program, the whole school or particular classes read or hear Eve Bunting's book, *The Wednesday Surprise*. Staff and an adult learner from the program then go to the school to talk about adult illiteracy, its causes, and its consequences. The children are always fascinated and surprised to discover that not all adults learned to read as children. They have many questions for the adult learners, who attempt to sensitize the children to the needs and fears of an illiterate adult.

The children are then given information about the library's adult literacy and family literacy programs to take home to their parents. A number of adult learners have called the library program for help after they received this information. On several occasions, a child has approached the adult learner and whispered that they have a parent or grandparent who cannot read. After each presentation, children experiencing reading difficulties are invited to talk to the adult learner about their concerns and problems with reading.

In another partnership arrangement, the family literacy program works with the Teen Mom program at the Pittsburg Adult School. The coordinator goes to the school on the one day each week that mothers have their children with them all day. She provides books, storytimes, modeling behavior for reading to children, magazines, crafts, games, and many other activities that promote language and reading development. At the end of eight weeks, mothers and their children go to the local library for a full morning of library programming that includes getting acquainted with the children's librarians, learning how to use the library, getting library cards for themselves and their older children, and listening to a special storytime.

The collaboration between the library and the Pittsburg adult school has resulted in improvement of the mother's reading skills and an important introduction to library services.

Costs

Part-time FFL coordinator	$24,000
Travel costs	500
Instructional resources	1,000
Gift books (plus donations)	2,000
Other	800
Total	$28,300

Various in-kind contributions are also provided by the library and other community agencies. Project Second Chance, Inc., continues to provide yearly donations for the gift book program.

Support Services

Project Second Chance provides one-on-one tutoring in almost every library location in the county. It also maintains an extensive collection of materials in most branches and major collections at the three primary literacy sites.

Special Services

Through an LSCA Title VI grant the library provides staffing for a computer learning center in the Antioch Library. The center is available to all students, but special times are set aside for literacy program families.

Project Read Families for Literacy

Redwood City Public Library
1044 Middlefield Road
Redwood City, CA 94063
Contact: Beth Parent
(415) 780-7077

Redwood City Public Library has developed a home-based family literacy program that features a unique recruitment strategy. Parents are referred to the program by the pre-school child's teacher, an outreach specialist in the schools, a counselor, principal, or other provider. After a parent enrolls in Project Read, the adult literacy program, the family automatically becomes part of the family literacy component.

Before deciding on a design for their Families for Literacy program, Redwood City consulted with several coordinators from existing programs. As a result of these meetings and Project Read's experience with low literacy parents, three fundamental assumptions were used in designing the program:

1. Low literate families do not normally use public libraries. They often find them uncomfortable and threatening.
2. Low literate families often struggle for economic security. While some low literate adults do have adequate financial resources, many work two or even three jobs to keep their families housed and fed. These parents have little time to spend on outside activities because their focus is on basic necessities and survival.
3. Due to a variety of logistical, cultural, economic, and environmental factors, there is little motivation for low literate parents to bring their family to a library-sponsored event—especially at a location they find inconvenient or uncomfortable. Also, because low literate parents rarely have found the library to be a "fun" and entertaining place (many go there only for tutoring), they don't think it could be an exciting place to take their children.

Taking these factors into account, Redwood City developed a 4 Phase approach that has worked quite successfully.

The library has made both Project Read and its family literacy component part of regular library services. Library Director Jane Light believes the literacy program is as important to the community as any other library service. Even in a time of extensive budget cuts, the library continues to support literacy services as fully as more traditional services.

Because of its close partnership with the public school system, the family literacy program has been successful in promoting more interaction between parents and schools. One parent from the program reports that since she joined, she has taken a greater part in following her daughters' progress. She now attends teacher conferences and enthusiastically helps her children with their homework.

Description and Approach

Redwood City is a culturally and socio-economically diverse community of 66,072 located just south of San Francisco. Median annual income varies from a high of $60,590 in the Redwood City hills to below $15,000 in Fair Oaks and the central part of the city. The minority school population has grown consistently, from 18.4 percent in 1970 to 59.1 percent in 1990. Most of the city's minority population is Hispanic. In many families, mothers are single or both parents work, and it is estimated that more than 8,000 children in Redwood City need child care services. However, there are fewer than 2,000 licensed child care spaces available. In response to the need, this single branch library has an extensive children's services program as well as a Families for Literacy program.

Redwood City has structured its 4 Phase model around in-home tutoring. Prior to commencing Phase 1, the family literacy coordinator visits the home of an eligible family to meet family members. She also looks at the home and the neighborhood and decides if she is comfortable sending a tutor there. These issues are discussed openly and honestly with the family before it is accepted into the program.

During Phase 1 the tutor goes to the home twice each week, tutoring the adult learner in basic skills during one session and working with the entire family on family literacy skills and activities during the second session. In the family session, the tutor reads stories to the family and uses related activities such as fingerplays, flannel boards, and games, at all times encouraging the participation of the parents. The tutor also discusses parenting, child care, nutrition, and other issues.

Phase 1 continues as long as the tutor and learner feel they are making progress and want to continue.

At some point during Phase 1, the tutor and learner decide that they are ready for Phase 2. The tutor then gives the family an informal tour of the library, introducing them to the children's librarian, getting all family members library cards, and spending time with them in the children's area.

In Phase 3, the parents, children and tutor attend a special family literacy storytime that introduces the family to the concept of storytimes and to the fun the entire family can have during them. These monthly storytimes are given by the children's librarian in the early evening. The tutor continues to provide both basic literacy and family literacy instruction at the home and attends storytimes with the family.

After completing the six-month cycle of Phase 3, the tutor and family usually decide that the family will continue to attend the storytimes as well as the ongoing tutoring. Families are also encouraged to attend weekly storytimes for the general public, which are considered Phase 4 of the family literacy component.

Methods and Materials

The family literacy program presents storytimes once a month for children, parents, and tutors. The atmosphere is fun, relaxed and friendly, but each session has a regular routine so that families are not intimidated by the unexpected.

Storytimes always begin with families and tutors selecting books, socializing, and getting settled. The coordinator welcomes everyone and introduces the children's librarian, who reads aloud to the families and talks about activities that can be related to the stories, such as puppet shows, storytelling, finger plays, and folk songs. Families and tutors then participate in handicrafts organized by a volunteer. Finally, there are refreshments for everyone.

The program distributes free books to the children at the monthly storytimes and during office hours. Tutors and families frequently stop by the Project Read office and select books to take home. The program is very generous in its book giveaways, distributing 30 to 40 books to each family per year. All children in the family, not just the pre-schoolers, are included in the book distribution program.

Redwood City's family literacy model has proven quite effective; its retention rates are outstanding. Since all incoming parents' reading skills are carefully assessed, the program can document that adult learners raise their reading levels an average of three years within their first six months of instruction. Over 90 percent of students and tutors complete the six-month program cycle, and more than 80 percent continue their tutoring beyond that period.

Taking the program into the home and making participation comfortable and easy seems to be the real key to the success of this program. Diane Hanson, a graduate student at Hayward State University, will soon complete a research study that measures the literacy and pre-literacy gains made by the parent and pre-school children of 12 program families who were tracked for six months.

It is clear that the training and commitment of tutors are also crucial to the success of this program. Tutors select the literacy program they will participate in during the initial tutor-training process. Those who choose the family literacy component of Project Read return to the library for intensive training in family literacy. It is important that these tutors be positive, energetic, nonjudgmental people who believe in the importance of early language and literacy development. They must be willing to spend the extra time required to work with an entire family.

Recruitment and Cooperating Agencies

Redwood City Elementary Schools are the primary community partner for the program. Outreach specialists and teachers from individual schools identify low literacy children whose parents may have literacy problems and refer them to Project Read. The library has also received publicity from the superintendent's office and support from the Parent-Teacher Association (PTA) for tutors and students. School newspapers often promote the library's programs through articles and announcements.

The Head Start program has made a concentrated effort to communicate to its parents the importance of reading regularly to their children and has encouraged families to participate in library-based family literacy programs. It has been a good source for referrals. In addition, numerous churches and day care centers actively recruit and refer families to the program.

Other recruitment strategies include advertisements posted throughout the library and the schools. Word of mouth has also been successful.

Retention strategies include giving free books to families and providing transportation by the tutor to the monthly storytimes. The children's librarian is also available after storytime sessions to answer questions about book selection and techniques to use for fingerplays and puppet shows.

Other effective retention strategies include monthly contact with tutors and families, which allows problems such as scheduling conflicts to be identified and solved as quickly as possible. As tutors and families regularly attend and experience the fun of storytimes, the retention rate improves significantly.

Tutor recruitment is the most difficult challenge facing the program. Many potential family literacy tutors who complete the regular tutor training program are overwhelmed by the idea of tutoring a family rather than a single adult. To increase family tutor recruitment, tutors are told that most of their effort will still be focused on the adult learner, and that working with the entire family will help adults to improve their skills.

Costs

Part-time staff	$17,500
Contract services	3,000
Office supplies	500
Printing	2,000
Instructional resources	1,500
Gift books	4,500
Total	$29,000

In-kind contributions of personnel and service were received from the library, particularly from the children's services staff.

Support Services

The library maintains a large collection of new reader materials and provides training and administrative service for volunteers who provide one-on-one and small group tutoring for adults. With an LSCA Title I grant, the library has established an after school program for at-risk youth that provides one-on-one tutoring. As part of the Families in Partnership Program (FIPP), the tutor and child read aloud to one another.

Special Services

Special services in math are available to families through the Family Math program. This program works closely with the family literacy program to successfully communicate to learners that math doesn't have to be painful and intimidating. Family Math conveys this message by presenting entertaining, yet challenging, math games to parents, children, and tutors. At six weekly family math sessions held in a non-classroom environment, the families have fun and experience friendly competition.

Conclusion

Although we are still a long way from having all the answers, we have learned much from our first four years of experience with family literacy programs. We are convinced that the library can be the catalyst that introduces and instills the joy of reading in parents who lack basic literacy skills, in their children, and in other family members. The library can serve as a nonthreatening, free, and enriching environment for adding books and reading to family life. Families can come to realize that books and reading are as important to their present well-being and to their future success as good nutrition and health care.

These model projects illustrate the variety of approaches in family literacy project design. New projects and established programs in both rural and urban environments have developed and succeeded in bringing diverse agencies together to address a common problem. The one constant that is vital in all of these family literacy projects is the collaborative effort among the team members and among community agencies. Through collaboration with other community agencies and because of a strong information network, the projects work and they work well.

Because lack of reading skills has a tremendous impact and affects so many areas of life, local agencies and libraries can successfully join together to try and achieve a community goal with long-term benefits for everyone: family members who read, who achieve and who participate in the growth of the community. Service providers and community agencies that have similar clients, but that previously had not worked together, have found a common ground in family literacy and the opportunity to forge new partnerships with their public library that benefit the client and the community.

Margaret Monsour received her MLS from Western Michigan University in Kalamazoo, Michigan. She has over 14 years experience as a public librarian and library administrator. Monsour is the project director of the Bell Atlantic/ALA Family Literacy Project. She has written several articles including "Forging Private Sector Partnerships," *Executive Update* (1990) and "Libraries and Family Literacy: A Natural Connection," *School Library Journal* (1991).

Carole Talan holds an MA in reading and a doctorate in education in curriculum and instruction. Talan has taught at the elementary and university levels as well as consulting for the California Department of Corrections, directing her own library-based adult literacy program and working with a program to provide literacy services to homeless adults. Talan is the family literacy specialist for the California State Library, working primarily with the statewide Families for Literacy programs. She has numerous publications, including a *Literacy Needs Assessment* (1987) and an article on family literacy in *Wilson Library Bulletin* (1991).

Forsyth Library